Femininity

A

WITHDRAWN

Feminist Perspectives from Polity Press

Series editor: Michelle Stanworth

Femininity

The Politics of the Personal

Barbara Sichtermann

Translated by John Whitlam
Edited by Helga Geyer-Ryan

Polity Press

© Verlag Klaus Wagenbach, 1983

Weiblichkeit. Zur Politik des Privaten first published 1983 by
Verlag Klaus Wagenbach. This English translation © Polity Press, 1986.

Editorial Office:
Polity Press, Dales Brewery, Gwydir Street, Cambridge CB1 2LJ, UK

Basil Blackwell Ltd,
108 Cowley Road, Oxford OX4 1JF, UK

British Library Cataloguing in Publication Data

Sichtermann, Barbara
 Femininity: the politics of the personal.—
 (Feminist perspectives)
 1. Feminism
 I. Title   II. Geyer-Ryan, Helga
 III. Weiblichkeit. *English*   IV. Series
 305.4'2   HQ1154

 ISBN 0–7456–0120–0
 ISBN 0–7456–0265–7

Typeset by Cambrian Typesetters, Frimley, Camberley, Surrey
Printed in Great Britain by The Bath Press, Avon

Contents

Preface

The personal is political: that was one of the slogans of the student movement. Today the problem is to prevent the last residues of public life from being treated as merely personal issues. In 1968 family life and love were removed from the protection of the personal sphere and placed in the hands of 'political discussion'. Today the situation has reversed and conflicts of global and apocalyptic proportions are tackled as matters of the heart. It is difficult to strike a balance between the conflicting demands of individuals and of the public sphere: should the concerns of each be treated in confidence or laid open to all? Perhaps there is no other way to proceed than by making corrections with the benefit of hindsight and by putting up resistance whenever privativism or public curiosity encroach on each other's territory or become stunted.

The personal is political: in the student movement, this was a demand which was made both by politicized individuals and by people who were more preoccupied with their own personal lives. They wanted to find a common framework which would enable them to analyse the processes of socialization that govern the inner concerns of the individual (in the double sense of controlling them and organizing them) and which would, at the same time, enable them to make changes in the outside world. It was a time when individual happiness was not expected to come about by chance or by depriving others of it. It was expected to come as a result and a reflection of a different happiness, 'public happiness'. Yet if today, by contrast, social conditions are evaluated in terms of how the inner life of individuals responds to them, there is still something of the spirit of that movement which knew that personal well-being depends on outside circumstances. But today there is no counter-move, no attempt to re-connect the enhancement of personal life, of subjectivity, to an 'improved' objectivity, that is, an objectivity which people are at least attempting to see through and influence. Private 'liberations' and improvements in one's personal situation are always desirable, but they seldom come free. If they are to be achieved with a clear conscience and with true conviction, we have to make an effort: the effort it takes to rectify the social conditions upon which private happiness or unhappiness depend.

The 'hard' political questions, such as war and peace, ecology and work, have always succeeded in mobilizing the public. The 'softer' questions, such as the critique of the family, children, sexuality and the relationship between the sexes, have either been swallowed up by the therapy movement or have disappeared behind a wall of nervous resignation. Only the women's movement continues to demand that the personal should be discussed politically.

No wonder. The personal sphere is something directly political for women because it refuses to leave them alone, because they cannot rid themselves of responsibility for personal matters. Women who want more than family life make the personal political – even without intending to directly – with every step they take away from the home. A woman in parliament or on a political platform is tantamount to making public something as personal as a female mouth or the hem of a skirt. The more that women outside the home make the world accustomed to their phenotype, the sooner people will stop equating femininity with personal life, so that it will no longer be the case that the personal seems political merely because a woman steps into public life. The most effective way to stop people equating femininity with personal life is for women's work and influence outside the home to be of such a kind that the political cannot be reduced to the personal sphere.

But we are still left with the personal life of emancipated women and women in the process of emancipation. There is still their personal existence to be considered, as well as that of other women, in so far as that existence gives cause for criticism and comment from a feminist perspective. Here too the women's movement has inherited the *élan* of '68. The movement still knows how to connect the intimate side of personal life to society, its history, customs, morality and politics, in such a way that by understanding how these things came about, the movement can develop an idea of how they can be changed. Making political discussions out of personal matters – from abortion to the concept of 'female sexuality' – is one of the greatest successes of the feminist movement. By bravely insisting on the political dimension of these conflicts, the movement has also made a necessary contribution to the preservation of the capacity for political discussion, a capacity which has been threatened by changing political trends and by the excessive privatization of individual unhappiness brought about by the therapy movement. But this changing context, this reprivatization of the personal and the consequent encroachment of personal demands into the public and political sphere, this inversion of the once political debate also had its effect on the women's movement and on the way the movement dealt with questions of personal life. The movement lacked and still lacks the opportunity to argue on a theoretical level. There is a shortage of people with opposing views to argue with, a shortage of people asking 'why?' in order to provoke the reconsideration and criticism of the arguments put forward. Thus, by the pressure of circumstances the women's movement came dangerously close to dull dogmatism in its plans and programmes. The women of the movement were, as I said, the least at fault: in the long run, even the most imaginative innovators can do nothing in the face of public indolence when their proposals are either accepted without question, stonewalled or rejected out of hand. When a social movement is successful – and the women's movement has started things moving in many fields – the number of serious opponents dwindles, but with them goes the chance to test out the ideas and Utopias the movement creates against an intelligent counter-critique. At the same time, this (relative) lack of public criticism is seen as an even greater success – while in reality it leads to stagnation. When things have reached this stage, there is only one thing to do: appoint a devil's advocate from within the ranks of the movement itself, make a serious attempt at self-criticism and present it to the public.

The ten essays in this book keep to one of the oldest themes upon which the women's movement has concentrated: sexuality. Here, in the most personal area, women have discovered their fundamental political essence. The 'small difference'[1] seemed too large to permit both emancipation *and* understanding with men, and it made it impossible for an independent woman to consider having a child. Is this still true today? Was it ever true? Is it not worth trying to give a theoretical defence of the love between the sexes and motherhood without sacrificing the very aim of emancipation?

After all, there is also a kind of 'private happiness' which does not rest on an uneasy compromise. The women's movement made a vehement and justified condemnation of conventional domestic bliss as women's only prospect. But what they put in its place – female solidarity – served only as a point of departure. There was no positive programme designed to include the other sex and children. This was hardly surprising, since to begin with the mere act of rejection was enough. But the time has now come to consider how the vast majority outside the feminist scene should proceed without being forced into a compromise. There are enough people changing the trend by becoming more conservative. To stop them, it is not sufficient to go on restating the movement's position and its integrity until what is dogmatic becomes boring to boot. On the contrary, that would be the surest way of losing everything. It may be that what we have to do now is to *approach the lion's den*, i.e. tackle the arguments put up by the opposition, which for us is patriarchal prejudice, the habitual lie of sexism, old and new emotive outbursts against female folly. Is there something to its arguments? Have we overlooked something somewhere? Have we suppressed certain fine distinctions or ambivalences? Missed certain ambiguities? We will only be able to tell if we take a closer look at the enemy – when I said 'approach the lion's den' I did not mean allying with the enemy, but fighting it at close quarters.

I believe that fear of being applauded by the wrong side has often prevented feminism from pursuing its line of thought. Pursuing a line of thought sometimes means thinking more carefully – and the sharper the distinctions become, the more certain we can be that despite its applause, the opposition will remain relegated to the other side of the stream of thought. In other words, if we risk proceeding from a common starting point and *still* manage to isolate the difference, then and only then will the opposition be visibly 'fixed' on the other side and left behind.

In my essays I try to take the other side as seriously as possible and to expose it as being wrong only when it is necessary to do so (but when it is, I make sure to do so). I also mention women's prejudices, the white lies feminists have had to tell, and emotive outbursts old and new against the norms of the man's world. If you remember that the only political formations which are always right are those which are dead, you can allow the feminist movement a few mistakes. At least *this* movement is still moving.

Notes

1   The expression 'small difference' alludes to a book by the German feminist Alice Schwarzer, *Der 'kleine' Unterschied und seine grossen Folgen. Frauen über sich – Beginn einer Befreiung*, Frankfurt, Fischer Taschenbuch, 1977. [Ed.]

morality and politics, in such a way that by understanding how these things came about, the movement can develop an idea of how they can be changed. Making political discussions out of personal matters – from abortion to the concept of 'female sexuality' – is one of the greatest successes of the feminist movement. By bravely insisting on the political dimension of these conflicts, the movement has also made a necessary contribution to the preservation of the capacity for political discussion, a capacity which has been threatened by changing political trends and by the excessive privatization of individual unhappiness brought about by the therapy movement. But this changing context, this reprivatization of the personal and the consequent encroachment of personal demands into the public and political sphere, this inversion of the once political debate also had its effect on the women's movement and on the way the movement dealt with questions of personal life. The movement lacked and still lacks the opportunity to argue on a theoretical level. There is a shortage of people with opposing views to argue with, a shortage of people asking 'why?' in order to provoke the reconsideration and criticism of the arguments put forward. Thus, by the pressure of circumstances the women's movement came dangerously close to dull dogmatism in its plans and programmes. The women of the movement were, as I said, the least at fault: in the long run, even the most imaginative innovators can do nothing in the face of public indolence when their proposals are either accepted without question, stonewalled or rejected out of hand. When a social movement is successful – and the women's movement has started things moving in many fields – the number of serious opponents dwindles, but with them goes the chance to test out the ideas and Utopias the movement creates against an intelligent counter-critique. At the same time, this (relative) lack of public criticism is seen as an even greater success – while in reality it leads to stagnation. When things have reached this stage, there is only one thing to do: appoint a devil's advocate from within the ranks of the movement itself, make a serious attempt at self-criticism and present it to the public.

The ten essays in this book keep to one of the oldest themes upon which the women's movement has concentrated: sexuality. Here, in the most personal area, women have discovered their fundamental political essence. The 'small difference'[1] seemed too large to permit both emancipation *and* understanding with men, and it made it impossible for an independent woman to consider having a child. Is this still true today? Was it ever true? Is it not worth trying to give a theoretical defence of the love between the sexes and motherhood without sacrificing the very aim of emancipation?

After all, there is also a kind of 'private happiness' which does not rest on an uneasy compromise. The women's movement made a vehement and justified condemnation of conventional domestic bliss as women's only prospect. But what they put in its place – female solidarity – served only as a point of departure. There was no positive programme designed to include the other sex and children. This was hardly surprising, since to begin with the mere act of rejection was enough. But the time has now come to consider how the vast majority outside the feminist scene should proceed without being forced into a compromise. There are enough people changing the trend by becoming more conservative. To stop them, it is not sufficient to go on restating the movement's position and its integrity until what is dogmatic becomes boring to boot. On the contrary, that would be the surest way of losing everything. It may be that what we have to do now is to *approach the lion's den,* i.e. tackle the arguments put up by the opposition, which for us is patriarchal prejudice, the habitual lie of sexism, old and new emotive outbursts against female folly. Is there something to its arguments? Have we overlooked something somewhere? Have we suppressed certain fine distinctions or ambivalences? Missed certain ambiguities? We will only be able to tell if we take a closer look at the enemy – when I said 'approach the lion's den' I did not mean allying with the enemy, but fighting it at close quarters.

I believe that fear of being applauded by the wrong side has often prevented feminism from pursuing its line of thought. Pursuing a line of thought sometimes means thinking more carefully – and the sharper the distinctions become, the more certain we can be that despite its applause, the opposition will remain relegated to the other side of the stream of thought. In other words, if we risk proceeding from a common starting point and *still* manage to isolate the difference, then and only then will the opposition be visibly 'fixed' on the other side and left behind.

In my essays I try to take the othe[...]
and to expose it as being wrong only[...]
(but when it is, I make sure to do [...]
prejudices, the white lies feminists h[...]
outbursts old and new against the nor[...]
remember that the only political form[...]
are those which are dead, you can al[...]
few mistakes. At least *this* movement[...]

Notes

1   The expression 'small difference' all[...]
feminist Alice Schwarzer, *Der 'kleine'*[...]
Frauen über sich – Beginn einer Befreiu[...]
buch, 1977. [Ed.]

1

The Inducement Myth
Feminist Discussion of the Orgasm

The history of the new women's movement begins in the early seventies with the abortion campaign. The abortion campaign was spectacular: it influenced the higher echelons of politics and mobilized many women. But it was only one branch, only one offshoot of a wider question which was, at the beginning, the real organizing force behind the women's movement: female sexuality. This question was given a turbulent and practical formulation by feminists. As well as reading, repudiating, arguing and travelling to congresses, they turned away from men, founded women's communes and women's holiday camps, and discovered their history in the power of prehistoric mother figures and in the beauty of female sovereigns in Ancient Egypt. The revolution they led was consistent and effective: it may have affected only a comparatively small section of the population directly, but it sounded an alarm for the wider majority.

According to the old patterns governing the sex act and the relationship between the sexes, woman and man had occupied clearly defined places as seductress and conqueror, but these old patterns foundered amid the discussions and actions of the women's movement. 'Penis envy' was exposed as a patriarchal projection, the penis itself was shown to be superfluous as far as women's satisfaction was concerned and the vaginal orgasm was seen to be a myth.

There may have been many motives behind feminists' refusals to comply with the wishes of men or, quite simply, with sexual tradition, and the bearing and rearing of children which society expected of them (and many new motives may since have arisen). Yet any such refusals would have been unthinkable without women's determination to convert the desperate search for pleasure of their late childhood, of their fantasies and dreams, into a real and tangible encounter with pleasure.

From now on, nothing would hold them back: not pregnancies, not children, not men with their degrading practices and their penises. Women discovered love for women, self-love, or they revolutionized their relationships with men as far as the men could stand it.

From the beginning, the women's movement has always taken care to back up its revolt, as expressed in theoretical writings and in the press, with biological and psychological argument. Thus, for example, it was claimed that, to judge by the design of her external sex organs with the clitoris as the centre, woman was simply not created to be satisfied by intercourse with a man. Or, as another example: the psychological inclination towards motherhood did not exist as a female characteristic but only as an ideology and as a dictate of education. Thus, in their search for pleasure, women threw off all the trappings of the generative function of their bodies, they liberated themselves from men, the penis, from fear of pregnancy and from fear of the pill. In fact, they were so unburdened it seemed as if they would take flight at any moment.

Thousands of women, myself included, owe a great deal to those heady years, the explosion of confidence, curiosity and self-knowledge *among women*. It is only while looking back in a mood of consenting solidarity that I consider criticism of the initial debate to be admissible, but also necessary. Of course, we are always cleverer with hindsight; but how much cleverer we become depends on how closely we dare to look into what has become of those beginnings.

Much in the feminist debate on female sexuality, on vaginal and clitoral orgasm, on 'penetration' and the ideology of motherhood was, I think, an attempt by women to catch up with the great sexual liberalization of the sixties and to reinterpret it for themselves.

So far so good. But the feminist sexual revolution failed to take issue with the weaknesses and errors of that liberalization. It did not correct them or even work on them. If anything, it perpetuated them. What errors were these? A great deal of thought and writing has since been devoted to liberalization in the sixties: one of the harshest and most pessimistic critiques must be the one which says that, along with the pill and the miniskirt, smashing taboos and making sexual contact easy have reduced one of the last bastions of pure – albeit far from conflict-free – human interaction to the profanity of the material world: sexuality as a consumer item, the partners now interchangeable, pleasure as a bit of fun, a cheap thrill which is forgotten as soon as you wake up the next morning.

There is no evidence to suggest that feminists regarded pleasure – which is after all what they were searching for – as a piece of cheap merchandise. On the contrary, there are plenty of statements claiming that it was precisely the superficiality and lack of imagination ascribed to men which was repellent to women in the sexuality played out in the 'old roles'. I am not concerned here with what women strove for personally, what they desired in a subjective way or what they experienced as individuals. I am interested in what eventually came out of this rebellion and the way in which it was started.

If we remind ourselves, for example, of the discussion about vaginal and clitoral orgasm – a discussion which arose from a small tract by Anne Koedt inspiring many consciousness-raising groups, discussion circles and even dissertations at the time – then it is clear that in this case, the problem has been given only a biological or technical formulation. Reducing the problem to biological or technical aspects seemed then to constitute a kind of release: 'At last,' women sighed, 'I know why I'm not being satisfied: my pleasure centre is in a place which the penis can't get to.' But this was release by reduction, a false release therefore. In reality, it was an escape, dodging the issue.

I want to stay with this example and use it to show how, by criticizing customary sexual practice, feminists were giving support to the general trend towards trivializing the sexual experience and making it into something quite boring. The above example also shows just how illusory and fleeting the 'new' sometimes really was.

The starting point is the orgasm: women did not experience orgasm and they had to find out why that was and with whom such an experience could be induced. Concentrating on anatomy seemed at first to simplify the problem, while, incidentally, giving support to that sparring partner, Father Freud, who had said that 'anatomy was fate'. Well, women wanted to take their fate into their own hands but – briefly and technically speaking – they made it completely dependent upon genital stimulation. Of course, tenderness meant a lot to them, but the orgasm itself was basically the product of clitoral stimulation. Alice Schwarzer once tried to explain that 'penetration' was ineffectual by pointing out that, after all, a woman with a tampon in her vagina during menstruation was not in a continual state of arousal: the vagina simply did not possess any reactive nerves. I don't want to pursue this argument any further (there are counter-arguments like, for example, the fact that the entrance to the vagina is very sensitive, and that vagina and clitoris form a single reactive unit in physiological terms). What bothers me is the fact that the discussion remained on this level at all, i.e. that women obviously really assumed that their ability to experience orgasm depended solely, or at least chiefly, on how and where they received stimulation. And their unfulfilled wait for climax was due to the fact that it was always attempted in the wrong place. As if an orgasm could be induced like an electric shock when a circuit is completed, or like delirium when a drug is administered.

What they had failed to take into consideration, I fear, is what differentiates sexuality as human interaction, however debilitated it may have become in the meanwhile, from sex as a one-night stand: the difference between pleasure and consumer entertainment. When an orgasm comes about it always has a *history* behind it, a history of desire and arousal; and if one lives through such a history, then *where* stimulation occurs is of secondary importance. If the history was full of passion, if it was wild, threatening, serene and painful enough, then the orgasm *comes* even if – and I exaggerate – it is the woman's big toe which is being stimulated.

An orgasm is the last in a chain of experiences, of images, dreams, longings and anxieties: all sensations which unfold outside the bedroom. It is the last in a chain of impressions, expectations, disappointments, surprises, looks and touches. It is not necessary for this chain to have been constructed exclusively by the two people who are making love: other people may have a part in it, and many of its links may also be inserted by the individual alone in the form of fantasy or memory. It does not have to be a long chain either. But it must exist, it must have a certain *significance*, and if it does so, genital satisfaction takes care of itself. If there is no chain, no history, then even the most patient and skilful stimulation of the clitoris will have no effect whatsoever, there will be no real satisfaction. Moreover, the same is true, *mutatis mutandis*, for men. In a word: the problem, the great, smarting problem which women have of not experiencing orgasm is a problem connected with the time, behaviour and experience *before* the event. It is the problem or crisis resulting from the *history* behind pleasure, i.e. from whether it has been possible for desire to develop. It is this history which makes *naturalness* possible in sexuality, this history which allows the body to enjoy its full rights, which confers upon the body a life of its own, a life which is sometimes unfathomable, but always kind to us.

It has always been possible to associate an ability to show desire, a kind of *confidence in oneself as the desirer*, with the male sexual role, even with all the changes that this role has undergone in the last twenty years. I believe that the fact that men apparently have much less difficulty in maintaining their pattern of arousal, from beginning to orgasm without break or interruption, has something to do with this confidence. As those who are allowed to show their desire, they are able to allow the existence of a history behind their pleasure, thereby making their pleasure real and letting it flow from their wishes and imagination into their bodies. The woman's part in this was to make do with the role of desired object: she had to show herself willing to be desired. At most, she had a kind of *confidence in herself as being desired*, but not much more. For many women, this role may have been able to accommodate the history behind pleasure as part of the range of activity permitted within it, but it was bound to become too constricting for the formation of such a history when women had won more rights, more opportunity to express themselves and more autonomy in many other social affairs. In a word, as soon as women began to emancipate themselves, this role became too restrictive. In this respect, the collapse of the old sex-act pattern was an inevitable consequence of the tendency towards so-called 'social equality for women', a tendency which is older than the new women's movement. It is more likely that the women's movement uncovered the wreckage from this collapse than that it brought about the collapse itself.

The question of sexual roles is, of course, more complicated than presented here. I have allowed myself a simplification which I can perhaps retract in favour of a small refinement. If sexual roles were no longer reduced and firmly set patterns of action and reaction, but instead, possible behaviour patterns with room for an array of variations, then both man and woman would have a bit of each: both man and woman would each be a combination of subject and object. If the roles were really so polarized that subjectivity, the ability to act, was the preserve of men alone, and object status the preserve of women alone, then the question would arise, why do men have an easier time of it as far as pleasure is concerned (if that really is the case)? After all, in such an arrangement they too would be lacking one dimension: the ability to be an object. The answer is that as the socially superior, 'more powerful' sex, men have always been in the position of being desired, over and above any particular history. The inferior sex can do nothing else but look up to the dominant sex, at least as long as the inferior sex does not openly question the legitimacy of this domination and does not rebel. Here we find a reason for the irritation which the women's movement has caused among men: suddenly it is no longer to be the case that men hold the status of desired object by virtue of their sex alone, quite regardless of their personal charms. But even if men really were limited to the active role, this would still give them a better start as far as experiencing histories – or history in general – is concerned: because the active role in love relationships includes options arising from the ability to make choices and all histories in pleasure and love are histories of a choice. (Certainly there are elements of subjectivity for women too in the old version of sexual roles. But it took a great deal of personal courage – or a particular social position – for women to assimilate their roles on the basis of these subjective elements.)

When the patterns of social relationships collapse, die out or perish in some other way, socialized humankind has a great opportunity to turn over a new leaf. In the sixties, sexual abandon rose out of that strait-laced post-war decency which is now romanticized, like a lark out of a dead tree. I mentioned above the critique which saw little more in this far-reaching dissolution of taboos than a debasement of sexual relations to a simple barter – a pessimistic critique indeed. I meant to show that this critique fails to bring out certain positive elements of real liberation from anxiety and guilt, elements which are clearly present when taboos are lifted. Nevertheless, the critique is justified in many respects. Perhaps we can say that lifting taboos was a reaction to a change in the position of the sexes *vis-à-vis* one another which had been in preparation over a long period. In other words, a general dissolution of rules, rituals and patterns began as a result of distortions and inadequacies within the old pattern. At the same time, all those who welcomed this process of liberalization, failed to notice the *panic* with which those involved rid themselves of their inhibitions.

The cause of this panic was the fear felt by both sexes in the face of women's emancipation. It was a fear of pleasure being set free. What would happen if women showed desire, if men played the role of chosen object and if the 'clearly defined places in the old pattern' suddenly began to shift, to swap around, to replace each other or to become more alike? Would the pattern bring about an equalization of those acting within it? And would the consequence of equalizing sexual roles not be that sexuality would gain even more power over individuals and that the tendencies towards madness, excess and anarchy inherent within it would win the upper hand, endangering the personal integrity of individuals and that element of predictability which society requires in order to function. In the face of these dangers and the fears they engendered – perhaps not always conscious fears – the only thing to do appeared to be to run on ahead. Sexuality and what happens to the individuals involved in it were to be exposed and made transparent. This was to be done by mass experimentation. The impetus as such may have been good, but it overlooked the fetters which individuals drag along with them by virtue of their conditioning. These fetters seldom permit them to run for very long in practice as fast as they are able to do in their minds or in a first spontaneous attempt. This experimentation was carried out at women's expense – the inhibitions and taboos had acted as a kind of protective layer, albeit scarcely recognized as such beforehand, around their restricted ability to formulate a history behind their pleasure. One reason for this was simply that these inhibitions and taboos gave women more *time*. The pattern broke up: not under the pressure of increased opportunities for women, but because of a general blurring and melting of the contours of those once 'clearly defined places'. In fact, the pattern did not so much break up as get lost. Sexuality became something altogether paler. Because it was now easier and less trouble to do, the chance of combining it with a *history*, of experiencing it as something out of the ordinary, as something 'quite different', as a leap beyond the uniformity and linear time of everyday life, was more remote than ever. The equalization process took place somewhere quite different from where the prophets of liberalization had hoped: if the latest research reports originating, like most great empirical investigations, in America, are correct, then the intensity of sexual pleasure as experienced by both sexes is decreasing. If people are unable to provide orgasm with a history it becomes dull and indifferent. Thus it really would be true to say that sexuality is the last bastion of human interaction. It *stops* paying out its pleasure bonus when the reward it gives can be induced just like any other effect; when the path of human interaction, of history and of particular histories appears to be the long-way-round and is then cut short. The orgasm which is not part of a history, of its own history, which is just going to be 'had' as you might have a lollipop, suffers accordingly. This could be one aspect of the 'post-histoire' of an age – of our age – in which time has grown so old and motionless that nothing new ever happens any more, history has given up its job. The post-histoire of an age when it seems that everything can be manufactured (i.e. induced) and has to be made manufacturable. In order that this may happen the differences must first disappear, the irregular, attractive part of individuals must be blotted out, and the only 'subjective factor' left is the arrogance of those doing the manufacturing.

There is no doubt that women had grounds to stand up for themselves, to say 'no' and to revolt in the field of sexuality. But they did not manage to see through the inducement myth and to transcend it: instead they surrendered to it. The consequences are grave. The sexes have grown further and further apart (first among the relatively small, 'mobilized' population, but also beyond).

Instead of the co-operation and discussion due to take place, women have retreated into women's groups and men into men's groups. Alongside there is a flourishing culture which serves to remove the differences between the sexes – unisex, male and female look-alikes, and a new camaraderie between the sexes in everyday behaviour – but this is only a way of avoiding a meeting of the sexes and it is therefore divisive. What should have happened did not happen: there was no practical and theoretical formulation of a culture based on female desire; of a culture based on the female sexual-subject role; and on a male sexual-object role which was not invested with the vanity of a socially superior being but with the narcissism of the chosen object. (The sexual-object role, often reviled by the women's movement, is a perfectly acceptable one, in fact indispensable as a possibility or as one element in a role; it is only fatal when it excludes all other elements and possibilities.) If a woman stood up in a feminist meeting today and said that she thought men were seductive and desirable, she would be declared out of her mind. Yet such a simple remark might contain the makings of a quite emancipatory programme: for women to rediscover pleasure it is necessary for them to meet the object of that pleasure, they must look for it and notice it. The way they search, notice and meet it will have to change and may take on a quite new form: the plans could be laid for a whole new world since at present there are not yet any predominant norms or cultural guidelines for shaping this confidence in themselves as desirers, a female sexual self-confidence, confidence in themselves as a subject.

This female self-confidence would presumably involve all the 'trappings of the generative function', a proud confidence in the ability to conceive, to be pregnant and to give birth as expressions of sexual potentiality. I believe that it is one of the greatest, more recent merits of the women's movement that it has started in recent years to correct the rash protest it once made against the ideology of motherhood, which threw not only the ideology but motherhood itself back in the face of the patriarchy. Certainly it seems as if the joyfully conceived children of the women's movement are the fruits of virgin birth. The penis is not yet the 'in' thing again. Since the old way is no longer possible, a step back is out of the question, and a new way on which the sexes could meet one another as subject–

object seems difficult to cultivate – things will stay as they are for a while. Yet we should stop seeing a 'victory' for feminism in this state of affairs. Instead we should take it for what it is: an expression of the anomalous situation existing between the sexes, of a general apathy and resignation. The positive opportunities which normally accompany such manifestations of dissolution, the chance to reformulate (the structure of relationships, morals, identities) are not being utilized to the full as far as I can see. Everything points rather to a defeat.

Then what happens if bringing equality to sexual relationships really does involve the danger I mentioned above, if such equality surrenders individuals to their sexuality with the inevitability of fate playing itself out in tragedy? Or, conversely, if the discrepancy in power and prestige of the sexes must be present if sexuality is to remain domesticated in a manageable way? If the dangers are real, then the emancipation of women is identical with the emancipation of sexuality to the point where it becomes an uncontrollable threat to human relationships. It could be that the enormous resistance put in the way of the overdue completion of women's emancipation originates from a collective and unconscious panic in the face of such prospects. But things do not necessarily have to turn out this way. It could be after all that people who know they can be satisfied, who know that they can experience a history, are capable of imposing limitations which would no longer be taboos because they would be free of their function as techniques of domination. Perhaps there is some sort of emancipation from sexual roles which does not have to be paid for by giving superior power to sexuality. If there is not, would it not be better for humanity to sink into sexual excess than to remain standing, hollow and lifeless, on the barren rock of 'post-histoire'?

2

Towards a More Modern Worldliness
The Desire for Children

Among the women who were approaching thirty towards the end of the most intense phase of the protest movement, there were some who must have heard something within themselves during that unwelcome period of calm as the revolt grew silent, something which put them in an embarrassing dilemma. They felt the desire for a child. They were suspicious of this desire and felt they were being taunted by the suggestions it made. Yet, at the same time, they *had* this desire as one has a preference or an inkling of something and they could not prevent it from taking hold of their imagination. What they refused to accept was not the child they desired, but the desire itself. And yet the desire did not loosen its hold on them.

We may be able to understand this conflict better if we move back in time. In those years, a Berlin women's group gave out leaflets at a meeting which contained the sentence: 'Any woman who wants a child in this day and age is the victim of capitalist propaganda.' The protest movement itself offered little in its theories and views which would have been much use in criticizing this argument. Basically, the movement talked about women and children rather as if they were 'talking about the weather' – as Ulrike Meinhof once put it in 1968. This indifference was certainly one reason why an autonomous women's movement came into being and *at the same time* the reason for its initial militant ignorance on the question of children.

On this point, however, the women's movement was only contaminated by a more widespread indifference to this question.

But the mistakes in the appraisal of the situation by the women's movement were more obvious and the consequences more serious than in the case of other speakers with an interest in the subject. The desire for children as it is experienced or, more to the point, as it is not experienced today, is still a recent social phenomenon and is as yet unexplored as far as its origin and effects are concerned. It has only existed as a 'free' desire, i.e. a desire with alternatives, for about two decades. Therefore we should not blame the women's movement exclusively for not being capable of understanding and dealing with the forces which fuel this desire.

It may seem strange to assert that the desire for children as experienced today has only existed for two decades. I shall enlarge upon this. About twenty years ago the contraceptive pill was ready for mass consumption. Let us leave the advantages and disadvantages of this type of contraceptive out of the discussion; the fact is that since the pill appeared on the scene, the discussion about contraception and knowledge of it have increased by leaps and bounds, as has the use of contraception in practice. It has now become possible, at least objectively, to realize Freud's dream of removing the sex act from its alliance with reproduction.

Certainly women, and men too, have always felt the desire to have children, yet they have always been afraid of pregnancies. But whether children came or not was formerly much less dependent on their subjective desires and fears, much less dependent on their motives than today. In times when contraception was inadequate and unsafe, it was pure accident if pregnancy coincided with a desire to have children. A hundred years ago, and well into our century, nature came first, the motive second, and the motive itself was not so much an individual one as one determined by socio-economic factors: children were needed as heirs to maintain the line and to keep wealth in the family or, among the poorer, rural classes, as additional helping hands or to support their parents in old age. In addition, conception, birth and death were at that time elements of a religious attitude to life: a couple with many children was blessed by God in the eyes of the Christian Church. And even if individual believers did not always share this view in practice, what we advocate would nevertheless have appeared to them as an outrage, sinful and presumptuous, i.e. determining for oneself the time and place of conception. We can still detect the deep religious roots of the desire for children in the expression 'blessed with a son/daughter' which has survived as a figure of speech but scarcely as a reality.

Even in our own century the old motives behind the desire for children were still in some way retrospective, even in those cases where they seemed to carry the stamp of individuality. Reproduction was basically a tacit obligation and, moreover, it was an obligation which very nearly destroyed many women. It was an obligation partly tempered and partly disguised by feelings of affection towards their offspring. People took having babies in their stride, sometimes silently pleased, sometimes just in silence, but sometimes in mute despair: *they had no choice.*[1]

Meanwhile the desire to have children emancipated itself from its monolithic existence in a religious view of the world to become part of a richly varied individual autonomy. Sociologists would quote class-specific differences at this point: let us leave that aspect aside in order to simplify matters. As knowledge of contraception was reawakened – it had once been widespread in ancient civilizations and before modern times began – nature and religious faith were pushed into second place. First place was given to the motives and desires of particular couples. Furthermore, these motives and desires were no longer retrospective, but anticipatory instead. Reproductive behaviour is from now on characterized by a wealth of active and intentional motives. The desire for children becomes a plan as well as a desire and in this form it is quite new.

The ability to plan when the desire for children should be fulfilled causes problems in some cases. What happens in a case where the woman wants a child even though her social experience and her political socialization warn her – directly or indirectly – against motherhood? It is therefore clear that liberating the desire to have children so that it becomes an individual decision can lead to conflict.[2] This was not the case before: after all, why did people need to have scruples about their desires and fears when what they desired or feared simply thrust itself upon them eventually anyway?

The emancipation of the desire to have children, with its liberating effect and with the new problems it causes, is by no means complete. After all, there are still regions both in Europe and in the New World, which have deeply religious populations, where traditional norms and morals prevail – regions where they know nothing about the pill but everything about the Virgin Mary. (We are not talking about the Third World here. The problem there is quite different.) The desire for children is undergoing a process of *secularization*: it is becoming something *worldly* and in so doing, it is changing its substance and effect completely. It is gaining power over reality. Where once it was a phenomenon determined by collective norms in the form of powerful institutions such as the Church, by tradition and by a real dependence on nature, it has since developed into a diverse array of motives which are increasingly being formulated by individuals. Thus the desire for children is becoming an *individual feeling*. And it finally results in a decision and fulfilment in those cases where the conditions of fulfilment are in the control of the person who feels the desire. When I say that the desire for children is becoming more secular, I mean that it is becoming more individual, freeing itself of the restrictions imposed by a dependency on nature and religious belief, becoming a 'personal matter' with individual variations, in fact becoming a personal *choice*.

In fact, religion released its hold on a great many people long before the pill existed, so the desire for children could have become secularized much earlier (like civil marriage, for example). But the process of becoming worldly involves more than just the retreat of religion from a particular field of social activity. There must be a new element of worldliness there to take its place and to provide new morals and new meaning. A precondition for the encroachment of worldliness on humankind's generative imagination was the 'separation of sexuality and reproduction'. More effective methods of contraception were required – in short, the pill – to usher in a secularization of the desire to have children.

The drop in the birth rate of the Western industrialized countries may have to do with the fact that the secularized desire for children is gaining a stronger and stronger influence on the reproductive behaviour of the population, the proportion of wanted children to the total number of births is increasing and that means, in effect, that the total number of births is decreasing. Women or couples who are able to make up their own minds about having children produce fewer children than the parents of past decades (and centuries) who were dependent on nature and chance. Nature and motive have changed places. The motive is the deciding factor as to whether reproduction will take place, and nature is only allowed to play a role later to make the reality of conception out of the reproduction option if it pleases.

So what are the new factors replacing fear of God and the hope of having an heir? What is the secularized desire for a child actually a desire for? Does it exist at all as anything other than madness, insinuation, propaganda? How can it be that a woman who rejects motherhood on rational grounds nevertheless feels the desire to have a child and is thrown into conflicts and self-doubt as a result?

One possibility would be to work with the methods of empirical social research and carry out a survey. It is my view that the results could be used for quite a different course of action: for an investigation into the typology and structure of rationalizations, pretexts and clichés. But it would reveal nothing about the desire to have a child.

For years, I have taken an interest in the answers given to enquiries about the reasons for this desire (the reasons for its existence or non-existence) and I have collected these answers in my mind. Eventually I came to the following conclusion: basically, most people do not know how to answer. Therefore they just say anything, like 'I want a baby because that's the point of getting married' or 'I don't want a baby because of the population explosion'; 'A baby means there will be life after my death' or 'Why bring babies into the world when the threat of nuclear holocaust looms larger every day?' You always come across the same versions from a collection of plausible answers which reveal something about the topography of public opinion but virtually nothing about subjective motives. The most credible are still the answers which really say nothing, like 'I want a child because it's something you just have to do' or 'I don't want a baby because I don't see it as something you necessarily have to do.'

There are exceptions (individuals who have a more precise idea of the motives behind their desire): since the beginning of the secularization process, certain population groups have come to enquire into the 'point' and the significance for their own lives of things which happen, and to study themselves. These are the educated middle classes, but it is perhaps among these classes that women in our century particularly have had more opportunity to do without marriage and motherhood and follow other careers than their grandmothers did, so that at least in the question of marriage, an element of planning, of choice, came into it. Moreover, 'education' meant ascertaining and articulating the motives behind one's own actions and the actions of others, a process which has its productive side, i.e. not producing motives, but 'differentiating them out'.

Yet even among these educated classes, it is true to say that in the relationships of the younger generation, the decision which is now really left up to them to make, i.e. 'Shall we have a baby or not?' militates against any general study of motives. Any consensus which might eventually be reached will still leave those involved unsatisfied or unconvinced. In the personal experience of those involved, somehow, somewhere, the question of the child is not solved in general discussions. A considerable part of the question remains unsolved.

The explanation for this is obvious. Now that individuals can really make a choice, they must find the justification for their decision within themselves alone. The existing cultural tradition lacks socially processed experience of this type of choice, it lacks compulsory 'rules' which individuals can fall back on. But if there were elements of a cultural tradition at work, this tradition is one founded by men; moves towards a 'feminist' morality are often quite repressive in that respect.

Yet anyone who tries to identify the 'unsolved remainder' runs into trouble. It would appear that the secularized desire for a child has not yet become quite aware of itself, as if it shied away from admitting to certain genuine driving forces.

Can we at least sense such genuine driving forces as part of 'free choice', though usually they cannot consciously be drawn upon? I believe we must assume that there is some source of influence which is relatively independent of external conditions. It is a source of influence over and above the parameters we see in play when such a decision is made (parameters which are sometimes merely superficial and sometimes the products of an existential awareness). This source of influence is the *body* of the woman experiencing the desire and its willingness to conceive and give birth to offspring. I believe that the body has a relatively independent and significant say of its own in the genesis of either the desire for reproduction or opposition to it. I believe that the influence of direct physical needs on the (secularized) desire for a child has long been underestimated or not recognized at all.

I could also say that the desire for a child has its roots in sexuality, in its own form of generative sexuality, or sexual procreative needs. That means that in the case of the desire for a child or resistance to the idea of reproduction, libidinal forces are unconsciously at work, that the desire cannot be justified in an exhaustively rational way. As a subject for surveys – be they official or personal – the question of the desire for a child really challenges the person questioned to exercises in rationalization and conceal-ment, whether she is aware of this or not.

Generally, rejections or affirmations of the desire to have a child are taken at face value; at any rate, I have never come across anyone who thought it necessary to *interpret* such attitudes and viewpoints (even those occurring within themselves). This has to do with the fact that the secularized desire for a child appears, in public and private discussion, to refer only to social conditions, thus comparable to something like the decision whether to take one's mother-in-law into one's home or whether to stand for the chairpersonship of a club. Therefore it is seen to be something which can be discussed rationally without leaving an 'unsolved remainder'. But if the impulses which set the desire in motion are not at all consumed in social and financial considerations and if the unpredictable, spontaneous, perhaps even unconscious needs of the body play a part, then this is significant not only for discussion of the desire for a child and having children, it is significant also for theories of population development[3] and any kind of so-called family policy intended to influence the birth-rate. It would appear then that the material inducements which are at present being discussed or which have already been put into practice by the political parties and the government in West Germany are likely to be extremely uncertain and limited in their effect. It would be difficult to control reproductive behaviour at all by political means, and certainly not from one day to the next.

I shall sum up my speculations in a theory. The move towards worldliness has made the desire for a child into a matter for individuals, but not a matter which individuals can decide in an entirely rational way. Where religious faith or compliance with the force of nature which was perceived to be eternal and immutable were once the non-rational elements of the desire for a child, sexual desire or sexual aversion and repression have moved in to replace them. Sexuality – whether as desire or opposition – has, of course, always been one factor in reproductive behaviour. But only after secularization could sexuality develop into a causal factor.

What are we to understand as the sexual nature of the desire for a child in concrete terms? I do not want to present what I know about this as something removed from the places and surroundings where I learnt what I know. I want to guard against making a rash or even mistaken generalization. The area of society and theory where I have come across discussion, talk, communication and fantasizing about the desire for children is in the women's movement of the last three or four years, a time during which the range of emancipation widened to include emancipation of the body. When the desire to have a child came up in conversation among us women, we talked about our bodies, our potentialities, the physical and psychological experiences which pregnancy and childbirth held in store for us. And conversely, when our curiosity turned to our bodies, our pride in them and the need to win them back for ourselves, the desire for a child arose once more.

What touched me was how this desire was formulated in the women's movement. It was clearly a *physical need*, and it was presented with a mixture of keen expectation, aversion, bold words and embarrassment. It was a need which seemed to have its own dynamism, its tides and ambivalences. Woman's desire for a child has a *sexual quality*, a quality which is not identical with those forms of sexuality we are familiar with as hetero- or homosexual coitus.[4] Of course, copulation must occur if the desire for a child is to be fulfilled, but the desire for a child is not the same as a desire to reproduce. In fact, there may be no such desire to reproduce. The sexuality involved in the desire for a child is, in my view, a different variety of sexuality, and now that it is recognized as a specific variety, it can be rejected much more readily than in times when it was satisfied blindly, as it were.

The connection between sexuality and having children is not only biological, but also psychological, and has to do with the participation, charging and arousal of the internal organs too. Pregnancy is a *physical* phenomenon: it occupies, takes over and transforms the female body. How can a woman react to the rumblings, palpitations, twitching and squeezing in her sensitive erogenous organs other than with behaviour which is available to her as the behaviour of sexual reaction? Or with reluctance and panic, seeing pregnancy as a physical violation like forced coitus (which does not necessarily mean that copulation seemed to be a physical violation)? Or with arousal as she would to a sex act she had longed for, experiencing the seed in the womb as a kind of satisfaction? It is simply not the case that pregnancy is merely a '*consequence*', that birth is nothing but torture or even punishment, and that all physical satisfaction occurs beforehand. American scientists have just discovered that the physiological, hormonal and muscular condition of a woman giving birth (from the increase in the pulse rate to the rhythmic contraction of the uterus) is very much like that of a woman in orgasm. They conclude that there was originally some kind of biological plan to make it possible for women to experience pleasure while giving birth. Well, analogies are not conclusive especially when they refer to physical findings. When the human race began to walk upright, the exit from the womb was narrowed by evolution thus making it painful to give birth and to be born. But – and this is one thing in favour of the American researchers – is the pleasure experienced during the sex act not very close to pain? What characterizes both sensations, birth and orgasm, is that they involve transcending the limits: the consciousness becomes dulled and the body is tossed and pitched. Whether this is pleasure or pain, you are somewhere else.

At any rate, one indication that the reproductive processes are no longer part of God's curse on woman and have now become potentially pleasurable experiences is the keenly fought struggle for humane childbirth, a struggle to reappropriate the conditions of pregnancy and confinement. Woman are now shunning schematic medical 'supervision' and the obligation to give birth as part of a piece of technical apparatus because they feel that by the mechanization and increasing technology of reproductive events, they are being robbed of essential psychological and physical experiences.

Sexuality in its generally defined form, as the sex act, can also affect the desire for a child. I remember the contribution made by a young woman at the Berlin Women's Centre about seven years ago. We were discussing the question of children, and this particular woman said we should stop talking about the shortage of crèches and landlords who are against children. Instead, we should think about whether perhaps we had motives for 'doing without' a child, motives which we would rather not admit to ourselves. As she said, 'I'm thinking about our relations with men, especially our sexual relations. Anyway, if you are really in love, you may toy occasionally with the idea of having a baby however unfavourable the external circumstances.'

A satisfying sexual experience always leads to a strengthening of self-confidence, a refinement of sensitivity, and often to a distinct practical and emotional sense of adventure. It makes those involved more willing to experience a physical destiny shaped by nature. It makes it easier for a woman to accept pregnancy even when her social and economic situation does not recommend motherhood. By the same token, a state of sensual reserve makes women refuse to accept pregnancy or to accept it with mixed feelings even when their external circumstances are favourable for having children.

Generative sexuality is mixed up with the sex act itself in more than one respect. In particular, the psychological images and the emotional reflexes of the desire for a child point to interference – or perhaps a common root – between the two forms of sexuality. Of course, the baby desired is always connected with a man, but it is also connected with the woman's own childhood. It may well be the well-known 'man equals child' syndrome, but there is also a narcissistic memory of the little girl who once was. Women want to hold on to these two feelings, yet they also want to produce an object of their own to satisfy these feelings. Some people may also want a child in order to avoid the sex act, i.e. a child (a pregnancy) to protect the woman's body from the intruder. Moreover there are contemporary variants: the desire for a child may also be a reaction to the over-exertion caused by the kind of emancipation which relies too heavily on adapting male values and is seen as a competitive struggle; devotion without the fear of being abandoned. What all these motives have in common is that they are all refractions or tonalities of a single basic sexual motive which realizes itself first as a physical sensation and purely sensual phenomenon, only then entering the mind of the individual as an idea, however hesitant, astonished or sure of herself the individual may be.

A pregnancy may be physically acceptable for a woman yet still be terminated for other reasons: the 'external' motives such as income, education and living situation may bring a quite decisive influence to bear. The *happiest* situation is one where the pregnancy is both physically acceptable *and* socially desirable. The *unhappiest* situation is one where the pregnancy is neither physically nor socially acceptable. This situation must be removed as soon as possible from the range of possibilities by making abortion open to all women. Lastly, there is the kind of pregnancy which is physically/sexually unacceptable or viewed with indifference, but which will nevertheless be carried to term because it is socially desirable. I believe that this *half-way situation* is still the most common, though its tendential decline, as a consequence of secularizing the desire to have children and the growing sexual autonomy of women is one of the (unacknowledged) reasons for the fall in the birth-rate in industrial centres. With the contraceptive methods available, women are allowing the sexual aspects of the complex desire for children to play a more decisive role than before, consciously, and frequently unconsciously. If this is indeed the case, the development and maturity of this specific sexual function offers another starting point from which to explain the falling birth-rate. It is conceivable that the psychosexual maturing process of the willingness to reproduce follows a characteristic curve which certainly varies greatly for each individual, but which on average reaches its peaks later and less frequently in a woman's life than is generally supposed, or than people are willing to supppose. As reproduction became less and less sexual and more and more medical women were urged to give birth at an *early age*; the counter-emancipatory effects of this have not been discussed as far as I know. The 'purely' medical arguments sound irrefutable: with women giving birth late in life, the risks of complications or damage to the foetus are greater. But looked at over a larger number of cases, these risks are minimal and probably not nearly as serious as the damage suffered by women – and subsequently by their children – because of premature motherhood. Nowadays there are raised eyebrows when women in their thirties present themselves with a child perhaps even without getting married, and are then happy with it. But I believe that this trend is more than just an exotic fruit of the emancipation movement. It could be an indication that more and more women are postponing having children until they have reached the point where they *themselves*, in body and in mind, really *want* to have a child. They are at last allowing themselves *time*, something which was not available under the pressures of their former role, but which is a paramount necessity if any desire which may arise and hopefully be fulfilled, is really to be their *own* desire.

Freeing sexuality from reproduction was something desirable, a progressive step made possible by secularization and its promise of earthly happiness. We are getting nearer and nearer to achieving this. And we now recognize a notable implication of this demand: if sexuality is freed from reproduction then it means that it is only copulation which constitutes sexuality, not reproduction. Reproduction would be a mere 'consequence' of the sex act. It seems obvious to suppose that the patriarchy had a hand in this new definition: for men, copulation, 'sexuality', is in fact the beginning and the end of their procreative activity and thereby an element of reproduction in itself. Perhaps there is no more fundamental way of expropriating women's sexual potentiality than by curtailing their grandiose procreative role, or, more particularly, the parts of that role which begin after the sex act, so that they are nothing more than a burdensome necessity, 'reproduction', pure biology, just another bodily function for which the reward comes only after the child is born though the child is not to be seen as a reward in itself and is supposed to have nothing directly to do with sexuality or vital instincts.[5]

To avoid misunderstandings, I would say the following: of course sexuality ought to be possible without conception and without fear of pregnancy. Yet the separation of sexuality and reproduction should not deceive us into not seeing that the separability of these two phenomena is one-directional. The opportunities we have had in practice to uncouple sexuality (the sex act) from reproduction have made us forget that, despite the fact that we can now have sex without fear of pregnancy, the desire *for* pregnancy, if it arises, is still partly a sexual desire (or it may still be). When freeing the sex act from its coupling with reproduction, we do not at the same time release reproduction from its coupling with sexuality. We want and can have sex without reproduction, but it is impossible to have reproduction without sexuality. This separation of the sex act from reproduction which only seems possible in one direction is the reason for the existence of unwelcome, surprising and conflict-laden desires to have children.

A word to those women who one day realize to their dismay that pregnancy, childbirth and life with a new-born child have suddenly become the stuff of their dreams, as happened years ago with older women in the protest movement: don't rack your brains for an explanation – this desire is older than any doubt. Fulfil your desire if you can and do without if you think you must. But there is very little point trying to find reasons for this desire. I have met women whose desire for a child became such a problem for them, or was made into a problem by the inquisitorial social environment, that the foetus, if it got that far, must have been in the shape of a question mark.

Since the desire for a child originates partly in our instinctive needs, there is little point trying to justify it – to oneself or to others. If I may offer a very speculative theory: it seems to me unlikely that nature would make such an important matter as the reproduction of the species dependent, or even potentially dependent, on the purely rational decisions of individuals. Nature took precautions: even with perfect contraception and a complete shift of social prestige away from large families, there will still be children coming into the world, albeit fewer than before, because not only sexual desire, but reproductive processes too are anchored within the structure of human instincts.

This has a certain significance for social morality on the question of procreative behaviour. We should take care with our judgements about desires for children and the absence of them, whether in ourselves or in others. For since they are desires which have one foot – or perhaps even just one toe, but that is enough – in our unconscious, in our instinctive life, the censure of rationality has only limited power over them. It is difficult to say how we should evaluate this fact. I find it quite a *relief* since in all cases where nature determines our actions, it is more difficult to impose social and political control, powers which we should be wary of. Nevertheless, social animals that we are, we act even as natural beings within the context of our culture and identity: our motives are not superficial nor a simple mental reflex of instinctive nature. However much nature may control our actions, we still follow certain rules. There are social norms and morals which offer support or set barriers before us even when we can do nothing else but act irrationally. No such morality yet exists concerning the individual desire for children, which is after all, a relatively new social phenomenon. The more emphatically we – women, couples, children – the grass roots – begin to formulate this morality as a tolerant, sympathetic morality which respects inner dependence, the more difficult it will become for the institutional powers to enforce their own interests, e.g. through population growth, the ideological revaluation of large families and the reconstruction of the traditional image of women, and thus to infiltrate our desires with their interests, destroying them or alienating us from them.

Notes

1   More precisely, the only option men and women had was to renounce sexuality entirely – as monks or nuns.
2   From Barbara Bronnen, *Mütter ohne Männer neue Beziehungen zwischen Mann und Frau*, Düsseldorf and Vienna, Econ-Verlag, 1978, pp. 52–3.

> In our conversations we kept returning to the same point: the reasons for wanting children . . . . To judge by women's experiences, it is undoubtedly a dead-end situation if you *need* a child to have confirmation of your womanhood, to patch up a broken relationship, or to feel loved. . . .

3   G. Heinsohn, R. Knieper and O. Steiger's book *Menschenproduktion.*
Allgemeine Bevölkerungstheorie der Neuzeit, Frankfurt, Suhrkamp, 1979. In
their treatment of the motives for reproduction, they present an
extremely rationalist, one might even say 'vulgarly materialistic' point
of view which in my view makes their treatment of the subject all the
more dubious.

> In developed societies where wage-earning has become widespread, offers
> are made to women which are designed to make motherhood itself a source
> of income. . . . These offers still come predominantly from private male
> individuals, but the state too is experimenting with maternity pay. . . . In
> both cases . . . it is nevertheless true that the likelihood of a child – allowing
> for contraception – becomes greater as the offer of remuneration comes
> closer to a sum equal to the cost of the child plus lost income. (pp. 239–40)

4   The following goes for women only. It is undoubtedly the case that
men too experience a desire for children but I would not presume to be
able to describe how they experience it. I know too little about it.

5   From Regina Scheider, 'Selfhelp', *Journal Frauenoffensive Schwangerschaft
und Geburt*, 1977.

> Women's opposition to traditional methods of contraception has for some
> time been gaining strength unbeknown even to the left wing. The attitude of
> 'I'll leave it to chance' is an expression of more than just a kind of *laissez-
> faire* resulting from being fed up of the pill. The controversy about forcing
> women to have children and the burden of children (based on the discussion
> of test-tube babies by S. Firestone) and about a positive definition of the
> ability to give birth and have children as a strength and potentiality of
> women has begun to leave the realms of purely theoretical debate. More
> women than ever have decided to have children and to live together with
> them.

3

Rape and Sexuality

Essay on a Borderline

In its discussions about rape, the women's movement indirectly outlined a concept of (female) sexuality which bypasses too much for it to be complete. Certainly, the subject in question gives cause to emphasize the *peaceful* side of sexual experience and expression, but we cannot leave it at that because even this peaceful side has an element of violence. Just as rape is an attack not just on peace but also on a woman's physical integrity, i.e. a plain violent crime like any serious physical assault, so sexuality is not simply a product of two bodies in harmony or an exchange of affirmations. It seems to me that there has been an implicit compromise on this point which was rather rash: a false, cosy sexuality where two smiling people fall happily into each other's arms. When feminists protest against the fact that rape is considered harmless, their protest is based on a false idea of some kind of peaceful female sexuality which could be summed up in the catchphrase 'If a woman says no, then she means no.' As long as this continues to be the case, there will be no clear dividing line between physical assault and sexuality.

Peggy Parnass tried to kick against the prick – it did her no good. It brought her a nomination as 'male chauvinist pig' in *Emma*, a rare accolade for she was the first woman to get one.[1] 'Is it not true', she wrote on the subject of rape, 'that we have a desire to be "taken violently" by a man?' Parnass might well have deserved a slight reproof from feminists for using this cliché, but she was on the right track with what she meant to say. Perhaps we do have such a desire, I thought when I read her article, but we ought not to devalue it in terms like 'taken violently'. I even wonder whether it is feasible to mention it at all in the context of a discussion about rape, for if rape is real rape there can be no such desire present. The more I thought about it, the more it seemed impossible not to talk about this desire, about this and about other taboo expectations, impulses, ideas and fantasies which our bodies have. Otherwise, it is impossible to locate the borderline between assault and sexuality, between crime and pleasure, which is what makes rape such a grey area.

Recently, my friend Esther told me about going to see the film *Mourir à tue-tête* (by Poirier), an anti-rape film where at the beginning the act of rape is shown from the woman's viewpoint. Esther was working as a lecturer at the adult education institute preparing young women for their lower school exams. They were unemployed, but had in many cases spent their lives in homes or in institutions. She went to see the film with the women from her course. Afterwards the group held a discussion. Repeating a common criticism of the film, Esther asked them if they did not think that the rape scene at the beginning of the film was too realistic and too aesthetic. Wasn't it a bit like a porn film even to the point where men could find that scene stimulating? 'Never mind about the men' said one of the women, 'I found that scene a turn-on.' 'The crazy thing is,' Esther concluded, 'I knew when she said this that I had felt the same way. But do you think I would still have realized it if she hadn't said that? I would have repressed it and censored it, as an automatic reaction.'

It has long been suspected that women's sexual fantasies include rape fantasies, that the idea of 'rape' turns women on as well as men; and it has subsequently been proven empirically. But after scientific investigation the interpretation has changed, thank goodness: rape fantasies are no longer considered to be evidence of women's elementary masochism but merely to be figurative transports, metaphors for the movements of flight and pursuit, hiding and finding, disappearing and reappearing and the feelings of curiosity and fear, pain and relief, deception and surprise which are part of 'normal' sexuality. All these movements and feelings constitute a ritual, a game, or a dance as it is sometimes called, where the consummation of sexuality is an integral part. It is in the various stages of this dance that we should look for those elements which will help us to draw the dividing line we seek.

If the dividing line between pleasure and pain really does

become blurred at times, if Parnass was on the right track with her theory about 'violence', then there must be an element of (potential) injury and violence in pleasure itself, or to put it in the classic terminology, non-perverse sexuality must be bound up with an element of sadism and its complementary form, masochism. I think it has long been known that that really is the case. But the (new) women's movement, which after all started a feminist sexual revolution, avoids the implications of this realization.[2] They have largely limited themselves to rejecting the theory of female masochism, a theory, which as far as I know has never been given a complete theoretical formulation, but was sufficiently widespread as an opinion to be a contributory factor – making the crime of rape seem harmless in the public consciousness. The Viennese sociologists, Cheryl Benard and Edit Schlaffer, have had the last word so far in this dispute in their brilliant treatise on the widespread masochistic man figure in literature.[3]

The discussion, as far as it continues at all, hinges on 'who does what': which sex is the sadistic one and which is the masochistic one? Women protest about being told they are willing to suffer, and rightly so, when you think what sort of justifications were built in to the bold theory that women enjoyed pain. But even the next step, claiming a bit of sadism for women – after all, that is what happens indirectly when women discover an element of masochism in men – does not take us far enough from the question of who does what. Simplifying, there are three ways of either solving or getting rid of the problem. First, sado-masochism could be rejected as being perverted, and therefore need play no further part in any discussion of 'normal' sexuality. Secondly, sado-masochism could be projected away from women and onto men, the heterosexual men getting the sadism and homosexual men the masochism. Thirdly – and the reader will have already guessed that this is the 'right' answer – we could allow ourselves to consider whether sado-masochism, pleasure derived from inflicting and suffering pain, is not an element inherent in a 'normal' individual's sexuality, an element which is part of the 'dance'. It is not gender-specific in itself and if it seems so that is because sadism and masochism were defined culturally and attributed to the sexes on a one to one basis. If this interpretation is correct, then it is worth examining more closely that indivisible composite of pain and pleasure itself which stands outside 'restrictive' categories such as 'male' and 'female'. By so doing, we will move beyond the prevailing categorization and its critique.

When I say that pleasure in suffering or inflicting pain is inherent in quite 'normal' sexuality, I do not mean that we are all repressed flagellants. I mean that in 'normal' sexual pleasure, in the orgasm, there is an element of pain. In striving to reach that pain we must be 'normal' masochists and in inflicting it we must be 'normal' sadists. (I would rather do without the concepts of 'sadism' and 'masochism' from now on because they are not quite applicable. In their narrowest sense, they are used to designate the pain experienced in the *pursuit* of pleasure, and not the pain experienced at orgasm.)

The pleasure experienced at orgasm does not only put the individual in 'heaven', it wounds that person too. All the paraphrases currently used to describe orgasm stand as proof of this: it is a 'little death', a 'fall', a 'transcendental experience'. This is nothing new but perhaps something which has been forgotten: we, particularly as women, and as part of a 'sexual revolutionary' generation, are as it were accustomed to expecting nothing but 'satisfaction', the release of tension, happiness and enjoyment from sexuality – so that we do not see the threat contained in 'fall', the 'little death', and the 'transcendental experience'. As feminists, we have come to the point where we consider this 'threat' as being something which men alone bring into play, and which women can – and ought to – avert, e.g. by boycotting the penis. The fact that this projection is possible throws light on the nature of lesbian relationships within the women's movement. A sexual relationship without 'militancy', without pain–pleasure, is something artificial, a nonentity.

About three years ago, the Japanese film *In the Realm of the Senses* (by Oshima) was showing in West Germany. It had made the headlines because of a grotesque pornography scandal which ended with the film being released anyway. I did not see the film, I was told that it was rather boring, but that is not the point. I know the story of the film, and it seems to me to offer conclusive evidence: a couple who, in a kind of obsession, dispense with all life and

communication outside their two bodies, need to die to assure each
other of their love; the woman strangles the man who himself wants
her to do so, while they are making love. Then she cuts off his
genitals which she intends to keep as a relic. (Apparently this is a
true story.) The motif of death in love can be found in the oldest
dramas but what differentiates *In the Realm of the Senses* from *Romeo
and Juliet* is that it concentrates on sexuality, doing without any
subsidiary action, or intervention from society, which could
provide a plot or any other social pressure causing the lovers to kill
one another. In *In the Realm of the Senses* death results from sexuality
itself, the dichotomy between society (or better, sociability) and
sexuality is revealed *within* sexuality. The 'little death' becomes real
death and the cinematic representation, if successful, would have
shown that there was an inherent logic in this progression.

I quote *In the Realm of the Senses* because I think it is possible and
necessary to understand the story told in this film not as a story of
excess and deviance but as a story of extremes. The extremes
shown in this film are representations and demonstrations of what I
meant by the 'pain-pleasure' or 'militancy' of sexual peace (of
satisfaction). Another good point is that it is the girl who inflicts the
– lethal – pain, thus placing the question of the dividing line
between injury and pleasure beyond the traditional categorization.

Of course, in normal cases the individuals involved do not injure
or kill one another, but they are aware of a certain 'threat' if they
experience real pleasure. The 'threat' – and this is a very important
point – does not come primarily from the partner, but from one's
own sensation of pleasure, from one's own body, and it is only
reflected in the partner. 'Only' is rather misplaced here, since the
reflection is essential. The role it plays is so great that even in
sexual interest there is an admixture of fear, or a kind of defensive
reaction. The latter can become very strong if the interest is strong.
Our pseudo-hedonistic culture cannot come to terms with this
paradox and insists on trying to remove the element of suffering
from the feeling of ecstasy in order to keep only pure pleasure.
Instead of enjoying sensual pleasure to the full, we pick at it around
the edge, the 'dance' becomes a little fling. If the women's
movement wants to maintain its radical approach it must stop
contributing to the domestication of sexuality by leading us to

believe that sexual peace will break out as soon as men quit the field or at least begin to respect an unambiguous peace code laid down by women.

The crux of my argument about pain and pleasure is that 'pain' is an integral part of pleasure itself. There is no gender-specific desire to inflict or suffer pain, but there is a threat of pain for any individual who seeks or finds pleasure. Having once been forced to admit that women too are capable of experiencing orgasm, the patriarchy ought to have abandoned the notion of an elementary, purely female masochism (and the complement of that, a purely male sadism). The fact that it finds this so difficult shows just how easily shaken this new belief in women's ability to experience pleasure really is. You already hear all kinds of provisos. 'Women may well be able to reach orgasm but – their pattern of arousal is more even. . . for that reason they want several orgasms. . . they need more affection. . . more feeling. . .' all this threatens to put too much pressure on men, making them impotent.

I am interested to see how long this list of projections and defence mechanisms will get in time. I would like to warn women that there is no use in singling out the 'flattering' things they attribute to us (several orgasms, more feeling, etc.) and turning them against men. These things are no use to us because they are incorrect. The more one sex tries to dictate its own conditions to the other in the field of sexuality – instead of seeing that there is only one set of conditions which apply to both sexes – the more remote pleasure becomes for us and the more scope there is for an outburst of violence which has nothing to do with pleasure. I'm trying to cut the Gordian knot with this argument: sexuality is bisexual, there is only one kind of sexuality, one form of it which is in each and every one of us. We are monosexual, but that says much less about us individually as sexual beings than was assumed before. I do not believe that sexual experience, the 'dance' in a narrower sense, differs very much from one sex to the other. Apart from the sexual functions connected with motherhood, which are the reserve of women alone, sexual arousal and sexual pleasure are the same, whatever the sex of the body experiencing them. It will gradually become clear that all the carefully fostered 'finer differences' (in the pattern of arousal, the need for affection) are consequences of the damage inflicted on each gender by the other, and not genetic codes. The explanation for men wanting to come straight to the point does not lie in any kind of greater biological or sexual aggression, but in a historically traceable distortion of their sexuality which has apparently made it difficult for them to follow a more roundabout route as a means of refining their experience of pleasure.

As for the characteristic elements which go to make up a ritual or 'dance', we can now go some way towards pinpointing them. For both sexes there are elements of withdrawal, refusal, flight and hiding. Yet since at the same time as fleeing from pain we pursue the pleasure bound up with it, there are also elements of venturing forth, resolution, pursuit, discovery, even aggression – for both sexes. These elements are played out not just in moving closer or further away from the partner's body, but also in moving closer or further away from one's own body. Certainly it is one of the most pernicious accomplishments of the patriarchy that with its restrictive categorizations, it made it difficult for men to pursue pleasure by way of flight and made it practically impossible for women to seek pleasure by way of venturing forth.

Of course, individuals tend to favour certain elements because of their circumstances and because of their biological sex. But are they tied down to these? Our culture with its characteristic belief that everything and anything can be 'manufactured' becomes remarkably dogmatic on the question of opening sexual roles to all. What is missing here in my opinion is just not imagination and experimentation to extend the traditional boundaries, but also the ability to conceive of a particular role element as ambiguous or open to more than one practical interpretation. Most qualities have a complementary side – which may well be turned inward or downward but which is no less effective for that. 'However you twist it around', mutters the enlightened patriarchy eager to learn, 'the fact remains that women are more suited to passivity because of their anatomy.' If women ask what that is supposed to mean, alarmed by the revealing phrase 'the fact remains', they are told that passivity is equated with the willingness to allow something they do not want to happen to them. The desire for domination which every dominating force has to keep alive has, in the case of male domination, brought about a lasting perversion of the notion of sexual passivity. Even if women do have a stronger tendency towards passivity than men – why does 'the fact remain'? It would only mean that women are more able to let themselves go in a situation, not that they are more easily overcome. How fortunate it is to be able to be passive when involuntary physical sensations rule the hour. Old Freud was better at dialectics here than we who think we have to come much further. 'It would be conceivable' he wrote, 'to characterize femininity in psychological terms as favouring passive goals'. But we must not misunderstand him. 'A great deal of activity may be required to achieve a passive goal.'[4]

What is the point of this long discussion for the subject of rape? A case of rape is only very indirectly a sexual act; it is, as the women's movement has repeatedly demonstrated, first and foremost a demonstration of power, of a will to assert authority and dominate, an attempt to (re-)establish male dominance by means of physical force, just like wife-battering. Using the sex organ in this act of violence does not make it a sexual act, but only serves to show that the rapist despises not just women but sexuality too and wants to dominate both. Confusing rape with the elements of 'flight' and 'aggression' in the sexual ritual would then be inadmissible by the very nature of the thing. It is the patriarchy which has suggested this confusion since time immemorial, and for itself it has been impudent enough to claim mitigating circumstances of sexual ecstasy in cases of rape. For this cold contempt of women and sexuality, it has deserved every kick in the groin it has ever received. But we are playing into its hands if, instead of redefining the borderline between violence and pleasure with reference to the element of 'flight and aggression' (pain-pleasure that is), we deny the existence of these elements. If we do that the patriarchy will go on using them as an excuse when it commits acts of violence.

It may well be that a woman says 'no' when she means 'yes', and it is just as likely that a man does the same. And yet they may not necessarily be hiding the truth. Their 'no' is a way of saying 'yes' for because of the double-sidedness of pleasure it is sometimes very difficult to distinguish a 'yes' from a 'no' – the one is expressed in the other and pleasure may be increased by mixing up, deceiving and confusing, provided these are 'honest' actions.

Yet in the final analysis it is impossible to mistake an answer of 'no' which is full of fear and expectation of pleasure, with the cry for help of a rape victim: and the fact that the patriarchy feels so damn sure of itself in this confusion is a severe indictment of the quality of the erotic culture which it has created – a non-culture, as nihilistic and brutal as a rapist's erection. Why are there not more men who are horrified by the concept of rape and that by treating it as a *sexual* offence, the implication is that men's sexuality is depraved to the point of being an instrument of repression? At any rate, the ones who do express their horror are on our side: the front against rape does not divide the sexes, it separates the patriarchy from its critics, female and male.

It is perhaps some consolation that by confusing the pleasure-oriented 'no' with the 'no' of desperation, the patriarchy has above all condemned its own sexuality. So there is nothing left for men to be defensive about. We could make a brand new start.

Notes

1   *Emma*, 4, 1980. *Emma* was the first nationwide monthly journal to come out of the new German feminist movement in the seventies. It was founded in 1975 by one of the leading public advocates of women's emancipation, Alice Schwarzer. Peggy Parnass is a critical journalist in West Germany, who became famous for her lively reports from the law courts. [Ed.]
2   Of course, this is not true for every feminist. There are exceptions, e.g. Mona Winter in Karl M. Michel and Tilman Spengler (eds), *Kursbuch 60: Moral*, Berlin, Rotbuch, 1980; Renate Schlesier in Brigitte Wartmann (ed.), *Weiblich-Männlich. Kulturgeschichtliche Spuren einer verdrängten Weiblichkeit*, Berlin, Ästhetik und Kommunikation Verlag, 1980; Maria Wieden in *Ästhetik und Kommunikation*, 43, 1981.
3   In *Der Mann auf der Strasse. Über das merkwürdige Verhalten von Männern in Ganz alltäglichen Situationen*, Reinbek, Rowalt, 1980.
4   Sigmund Freud, *Gesammelte Werke*, Frankfurt, S. Fischer, 1961, vol. 15, p. 123.

4

Beauty, Democracy and Death

Before it was dealt a death blow by Betty Friedan in her book *The Feminine Mystique*, the image of the ideal woman had advocated more than just domesticity and motherhood; women also had to be attractive. Any woman who conformed to her role as a woman was supposed to be a good little housewife, but in addition she was expected to look good. This was something new compared with the traditional cliché of being chained to the kitchen sink. Once they were hitched, our grandmothers could look however they wanted, provided they did not fail in their duties as wives and mothers. Beauty played no part; in fact, it was viewed with suspicion. The same was true for the older generation of today. It was the 'feminine mystique' of the fifties which first made attractiveness an obligatory attribute for *every* woman rather than just for the exceptional case such as the model or film star. The modern house-wife of the prosperous post-war period not only had to clean kitchen floors and children's noses, she also had to smarten up her own appearance. And she was supposed to be not just pretty and smart, but as far as possible, *sexy* and of course, *young-looking* at any age.

So when this feminine mystique, which condemned careers and education for women as 'unfeminine' and damaging, was recognized for what it was, the pressure to look good was quite logically in the firing line for criticism. Women of various age-groups and professions, and even male authors with enough sensitivity to recognize veiled forms of discrimination, turned vehemently against the idea of attractiveness dictated by the media, the fashion industries and corrupt public taste. In America, Women's Libbers burned their bras and bombed beauty contests. Many older women stopped belying their years with hormone creams, peroxide or face-lifts: why not show off wrinkles and grey hair, the traces of a life

lived, signs of being alive with a charm of their own? Fashion
followed the emancipation and became anarchic: you could wear
anything, any skirt-length, any colour, any style. Jeans became pre-
eminent among clothes for both sexes and conquered the world.
Certainly, jeans were primarily a symbol of rejection – rejection of
careerism and discipline – among the *younger* generation, as was long
hair for men. Yet they also reflected the emancipation of younger
women from the ideas, held by their parents' generation, of what a
woman should be. This was above all emancipation from the
pressure to be pretty and 'smart' in a feminine way.

Within the women's movement, the question of how you looked
and what you did to your outward appearance had always been a
topical and controversial one. Women agreed that wearing make-
up, dressing smartly and so on involved an element of pressure: a
woman does these things because it is expected of her, and because
by now, she can't help doing it. But does she really want to help it?
It may be a great relief for a woman just to forget the curlers,
deodorant and depilatory creams and to go her unkempt way as
God created her. On the other hand, many women really get a lot
of fun out of putting on make-up and jewellery and doing their hair,
and discussion evenings in the women's group have quite often
ended with the women swapping their blouses and putting each
other's hair up.

The question is, where does the voluntary fun end in these
activities and where does the pressure to conform begin? At what
point are we beginning to bow to the pressure to disguise our
individual appearance in a 'corrective' way? We also have to
interpose another question: why is it only women who are
encouraged to make themselves beautiful, why are they called the
'fair sex'?

The connection is basically quite simple: in a society like ours
where the key positions of social power and influence are held by
men, women only gain a measure of prestige, success and influence
if they are accepted by men. And being accepted by men always
involves the sexual element, since the relationship of domination
considered here is a relationship existing between the *sexes*. To
simplify, we may put it as follows: men have shared out the world
between them, or at least, they have shared out anything of

interest, the 'world' in its emphatic sense, the external world. Political and economic power, productive work, science, art and other public fields of activity are the domain of men. All that is left for women is one sphere which has always been theirs – the sphere of the sexual element itself. And within this sphere, the charm which one sex holds for the other is a kind of *power*. In that phrase 'the fair sex', fairness, or beauty, is a cipher for *the* power, the only power, which women may possess. It is a cipher for the reduction of women's prospects in life to this sexual element. Yet even in the heyday of the patriarchy this reduction was never totally successful, though it can still be felt as a tendency today, when women have long since been competing with men for positions and public influence.

How then are we to deal with *the* power which the patriarchy grants us (and which it must grant us for its own edification), i.e. beauty? I should mention here that in reducing women to a purely sexual role, the patriarchy has not always allowed women to wield the power of beauty. There were and are societies and cultures which demanded that women forsake their charms to be able to bear children and bring up a family (which is, if I might put it like this, the 'hard core' of sexual existence). We only have to think of Victorian prudery or the Muslim veil. But in those cases where the female art of seduction is socially recognized or even demanded, is it then compatible with emancipation? Would it not be more consistent – for us now – to reject totally our role as a feast for the eyes of the dominant male sex?

Or is there a certain emancipatory potential concealed within this encouragement to be beautiful? After all, do we really want to become Victorian women again, or even go around in veils? Would it not be true to say that any shift in women's sexual role towards the art of seduction, eroticism, flirtation and narcissism may be interpreted as a relative step towards freedom compared with being tied to traditional domesticity? Surely the role of desired loved-one permits a greater subjective element than that of housewife? It depends. The question is, do the prevailing rules of the '*ars amandi*' allow women any kind of subjectivity? What goes to make up the particular images which women are supposed to live up to?

It is well known that beauty and attractiveness are relative concepts. But whatever the image of the beautiful woman at a particular time, in a patriarchal society it mirrors the dreams and wishes of men. The 'feminine mystique' of the fifties intended women to be super-sexy, passive and sensual in a childlike way. I remember the American and Italian film stars of that era: they were called 'sex goddesses' and 'sweater girls', and people said they envied each other every inch of their bust measurements. It is not difficult to pick out reductive and counter-emancipatory elements inherent in this ideal of woman. The whole 'feminine mystique' was after all part of a move to restore the patriarchy, a move against the great wave of emancipation which took place in the first decades of our century and against the self-reliance which women had in a way been forced to acquire during the Second World War. Marilyn Monroe was the patriarchy's answer to Bette Davis, Barbara Stanwyck and Marlene Dietrich. Now they were back home from the war, men wanted women to vacate their jobs and public functions for them. They wanted women to be 'all woman' again and they wanted to recover from war and emancipation in the arms of a consenting wife or girlfriend. And so in their images of ideal women, they blew up the characteristics of consenting femininity (large breasts, the 'curves') and of a passive, infantile sensuality (pouting lips, chirping voice) into so-called 'over-idealized show pieces'. Women were supposed to show 'everything they had', which in practice meant they were allowed to show nothing more than their sexual attributes. Any possibility of emancipation there may have been in emphasizing the role of lover was all but lost because of the reductive way in which this role was formulated. The attractive woman under the spell of the 'feminine mystique' was really nothing but a sex object in the worst sense. As far as woman's appearance was concerned, the aesthetics of sexual attraction could only be seen as the aesthetics of submission.

This ideal of beauty demanded a substantial element of surrender, not just from girls without baroque figures, but from *every* woman. This was firstly because the ideal was so rigid (the attractive type was defined narrowly and permitted little deviation) and secondly, because expressing the ideal consisted precisely of aestheticizing surrender. Marilyn Monroe was an embodiment of the fifties' ideal of beauty: she was an embodiment of *surrender*, and she became increasingly successful at this as she found it more and more difficult, contrary to appearances, to surrender herself. Within the aesthetics of submission, surrender at a high cost is more attractive. It is no mystery that Marilyn Monroe eventually died because of the demands of her social role.

There is another prominent victim of the 'feminine mystique' from that period, a representative of the other extreme within a typology of female talents: Sylvia Plath, who did not succeed in tearing herself away from the demands of the feminine mystique. She felt *compelled* to marry an authoritarian man and have children. She felt compelled to be attractive, adroit and up to the mark as a mother and housewife while *at the same time* exposing the lies inherent in this idyll in her capacity as a poet and novelist. Just like Marilyn Monroe, she was unable to live the lie and expose it at one and the same time and eventually she killed herself.

Of course I am not claiming that those two women died as a direct result of demands for beauty inspired by 'the feminine mystique'. But I believe that these demands were of great significance for their lives and eventually for their deaths. Beauty is not just relative in the sense that it is a question of taste which every individual faces in a different way. In its concrete form, it is also subject to social influences which impress themselves very powerfully upon us. It is often difficult or even impossible for individuals to evade these influences, and it is especially so for women since the question of attractiveness and beyond that, the question of sexual *imago*, play a very significant part in their everyday lives.

Let us return to the question we asked before, i.e. to what extent do efforts to adorn and beautify constitute a justified, voluntary, 'good' impulse and to what extent do they represent a forced reaction to the dictates of society? We may now go some way towards answering this question by saying that when women make themselves beautiful they are accepting their role as sexual beings; indeed, they are emphasizing this sexual side of themselves. This must always entail a certain amount of conformity with the prevailing allocation of social roles. 'Adorned women' comply with society's expectations, but they do not necessarily comply with being *confined* to the purely sexual role. A beautiful woman or a woman who likes to make herself look beautiful may also be an entirely successful career woman and still oppose being reduced to her biological function. But usually, changing or beautifying the outward appearance is a way of conforming to a prevalent ideal, and it mainly depends on the character of this ideal whether this act of conformity can be seen as perfunctory broadening or repressive restriction of female individuality.

In the sixties, the decade of international youth protest, the sex goddesses were toppled and their place as the ideal was taken by a different kind of woman. She was still attractive in a youthful way, but it was a self-confident attractiveness and was sometimes androgynous. Faye Dunaway, Julie Christie or Vanessa Redgrave would not have stood a chance in the international film industry ten years earlier. As for women who made themselves look beautiful, their efforts were now rewarded with more than just self-denial. This was because the ideal of beauty became more diffuse, allowing and even encouraging features of individuality. Self-denial was no longer a factor implicit in the ideal. Instead, the new ideal granted women autonomy and credited them with minds of their own. Even though the realm of desire and images was still constructed around sexuality, women were now supposed to have an element of subjectivity and needs of their own.

However, there was still a legacy of the 'feminine mystique' in the sixties, a fatal legacy which, as far as I know, went unnoticed as such until it was questioned by the new women's movement in the seventies. This was the fact that the encouragement to be beautiful still extended to *all* women. If the pressure to be beautiful is not to be a burden and 'outside the realm of domination', to put it rather dramatically, it is not enough for the ideal of beauty to be generous and not demand surrender. The social pressure to be beautiful must not apply to everyone, beauty must not be *obligatory* for all. In other words, the pressure to be beautiful must not be applied indiscriminately to all women. Making oneself beautiful is only fun if one is *free to choose* this kind of sexual existence which involves narcissism and seduction as a 'way of life', instead of being forced to lead that kind of existence as the only possibility open to one. More and more women are now refusing to be tied down to this sexual existence in spite of social pressure, and they are looking for their own path to follow. But it is not easy for them, because people nearly always see their path as a detour which will eventually lead back to the sexual existence they are 'really' looking for. Evidence of this is the fact that most working women are still expected to be 'well turned out'. Dear professional woman reader, what happens if you oversleep one morning: do you not bother to do your hair, or do you go without breakfast? If you go without breakfast, do you not agree that there is an element of self-denial involved there?

The reason why the dictates of attractiveness continue to apply to all women (a dictate is only a dictate if it is applicable to all) is, according to feminist polemics, because we have not yet seen the end of patriarchal culture. I do not think this explanation is comprehensive enough. As I have already pointed out, the patriarchy has gone both ways in the course of its history. At times it has forced women into displaying feminine charms, while at other times it has forbidden them to do so. So we must turn our thoughts in other directions.

The fact that women were urged to 'look after themselves' and that people got the mistaken idea that the privilege of being beautiful could be available to all is, in my opinion, the result of the great *waves of democratization* seen in our century, and particularly the effects this process had on culture and consumerism, as witnessed in the mass media and mass consumption. This material democracy besides a purely political one required that elements of luxury should be brought within the reach of everyone on the level of mass consumer goods. Cars, houses and champagne were to be available to everyone, or at least to the majority, and likewise physical beauty promised to pay its tribute to democracy by descending from the salons and catwalks into the living-rooms of the great urban populace. At last, silk stockings, high-heel shoes and lipstick, classic requisites of the female art of seduction, were available cheaply in the towns as mass-produced articles. And the cinema allowed even the poorest working-class woman to get hold of detailed information on the attributes which made up the prevailing ideal of beauty.

And women rush out and buy all this paraphernalia. So what of the men? We know from representative surveys that good looks come high on men's list of qualities for the ideal partner. The whole world seems to be obsessed with feminine charms, with women supplying and men demanding. And the tragic part of this situation is that the commodity in question, which every woman would like to be able to supply and every man enjoy, is in fact in very *short supply*. Beauty is as rare as a black swan. And an even more modest attractiveness, such as a pretty face or 'good figure', which merits a second look on the bus or in the pub, does not distinguish the majority of women. The *raison d'être* of beauty, even modest beauty, seems to be its rarity. If beauty was a feature as common as arms and legs it would go unnoticed, thus making a nonsense of all the longing, myth and untruth surrounding the real or supposed possibility of attaining it.

Beauty cannot be democratized. That is the embarrassing fact for a culture and policy which find their justifications in making all the desirable commodities of this world accessible to all. Many of the epoch-making promises of democracy were actually fulfilled. It promised people a share in political decision-making and it promised them a share in the good things of life. But many of these good things it could not possibly give them, objectively speaking, and by doing so the things lost their value and became insubstantial.

I am not saying anything against political democracy here. But despite all the advantages which it has brought us, its cultural and consumerist sides have led us into a morass of problems. We are all familiar with the problems caused by cars and even the tendency towards home-buying has had ambivalent results: it makes people immobile and narrows their horizons. And beauty? The promise contained in the advertisement which says 'Any woman can be beautiful' is a blatant lie – but people do not realize this if they have forgotten that once beauty, or the power it bestows, is open to all, it lacks any substance.

So if good looks really are rare but we pretend they are generally available – as an attribute for women and as a consumer commodity for men – what will happen to us now that we have fallen for this deception? It is inevitable that a creeping frustration will spread, coupled with frantic, constantly renewed and constantly fruitless attempts to grasp the desired commodity all the same. Aesthetic perception will become corrupt and will concentrate only on those features which really can be altered or 'corrected'. People will forget that other factors play a role in sensual attraction between the sexes over and above the outward effects achieved through clothes and make-up. The aesthetics of sexual attraction will be reduced to a kind of façade aesthetics. Women's willingness to present themselves for inspection and men's willingness to look and judge will revolve more and more around artificial 'window dressing', the illusion of beauty. Finally, a perfect façade will rule out physical contact because it will be too brittle. Sensuality will be limited to the remoteness of looking. At that point, men will only get their enjoyment if they put up their own façade. The result is a kind of narcissistic dance, devoid of attraction or contact, in which each individual communicates with his or her own façade and nothing more. The so-called disco scene is a blatant demonstration of this trend.

I mentioned at the beginning of this chapter that the women's movement has expressed theoretical and active opposition to the dictates of attractiveness. This began about ten years ago and has continued to be effective, even giving rise to the new Fat Movement in the USA. Public opinion has also become more receptive to the resistance women are putting up in the face of constricting pressure to be fashionable and young-looking. These moves away from the conformism of façade aesthetics are very welcome, but I think something is missing. We rely on the illusion of beauty to convince ourselves that true beauty is not so rare. So doing away with this illusion should be a rather painful experience. What I see as missing is a feeling of regret at the disappearance or remoteness of beauty. The women who are liberating themselves from the dictates of attractiveness have no such feeling. Even if beauty cannot be manufactured or made available to all, I still think that a longing for beauty is deeply rooted in most of us. Beauty is one of the foremost objects of our desire on a par with wealth or power. Even if we cannot have it ourselves we constantly feel a desire at least to *see* beauty, and we ought at times to show a little sorrow if we do not posses beauty ourselves or if we cannot have it around us constantly. Instead of consoling ourselves with the lie that beauty is readily available at any time or not at all important, we ought to get used to the fact that this is simply not the case, with all the sorrow and regret that that involves.

I have noticed that the statements of protest coming from many women against the pressure to look good sound so *cheerful*. 'We old people', the old women say, 'show off our grey hair and our wrinkles: we think we are beautiful as we are'. 'We fat people' say the fat people, 'we couldn't give a damn about all this dieting and massage business, we're proud of being fat. Who says fat isn't beautiful?' 'We knock-kneed women', say the emancipated women with quite normal flaws, 'we women with breasts which are too big or too small, we women with fat bottoms and big noses, we accept ourselves as we are and we think we're just fine as we are.' And then in a magazine where this kind of thing appears, we see a picture of an old, fat or big-nosed woman beaming out at us. She accepts herself and so she is happy, her happiness shines out of every pore. 'And so it should be', we think and we are happy too. After all, women who have freed themselves from the dictates of attractiveness really do look better than the lady teetering along painfully in high-heels who has something pitiful about her simply because she is afraid of what she looks like.

I am impressed by this new self-confidence among unattractive and old women. But there must be that element of sorrow there if this kind of emancipation is to last, if it is to be more than just temporary euphoria. We want to get away from externals, yet we have to admit to ourselves that externals – physical beauty and attractiveness – are extremely important for us as human beings because of the extent to which we crave visual stimulation. Given this fact, the only way human beings will get away from the aesthetics of illusion is by *coming to terms* with the fact that youth and beauty are transitory or in short supply. I cannot see that the feminist critics of the dictates of attractiveness or the members of the Old and Fat Movements are looking for ways of coming to terms at all. Instead they seem to be disputing the fact that it is necessary to do so by simply turning fatness and old age into acceptable varieties of attractiveness, or worse, by repressing their longing for beauty altogether. Emancipation on those terms cannot last. What we repress comes to the fore again sooner or later – that much we now know.

By excluding our longing for beauty from our self-perception we may be shutting out even more – notably, our fear of death. Life and beauty are as closely related as beauty and youth. It is only very rarely that age and beauty go hand in hand. The goddess of beauty, opportunist that she is, prefers to inhabit a young body.

Recently I saw a television programme about Douglas Sirk, a film director who emigrated from Austria to the USA. The director talked about the stars he had worked with and the actors were interviewed about their work with Sirk. The interviews were interspersed with scenes from Sirk's films made more than thirty years ago. So we saw Rock Hudson and Dorothy Malone as they are today, aged about sixty, being interviewed by the man making the programme and we saw them in those old films as young stars. The contrast was constantly reinforced and I had plenty of time to get a good look at the close-ups from the old films and to study the faces of the now-ageing stars being interviewed. I made a spontaneous attempt to adopt the humane aesthetics of emancipation and to tell myself that the wrinkled, smiling faces of these one-time stars telling their life stories were 'beautiful' – perhaps even more beautiful than the clear faces of their youth.

But I could not convince myself. What I actually *felt* when one film excerpt finished and the old faces returned to the screen was horror. I found the editing cruel. What they glossed over, yet showed up clearly in the immediacy of the contrast, was the *destruction* wrought by time on the once strikingly clear features of these stars. Time had felled an angel and a nymph, broken a spell – how else was I to perceive its power than with horror? Between the images on the screen, the programme told the story of a death; the death of beauty which had gone hand in hand with youth. Instead of concentrating on how expressive these old faces were as the aesthetics of emancipation would have demanded, I found it more appropriate to mourn the passing of the young faces. I realize I am dramatizing this a little, but I would like to make it clear what powerful emotions are involved in longing for beauty and lamenting the loss of it or the difficulty of achieving it.

Maryse Holder, an American who let herself be driven to a kind of 'death in Venice' by the lures of Mexican beaches and the young people there, recently documented the violence of this emotion. Maryse Holder was an intellectual but she was unable to content herself with the sublimated forms of her longing. She wanted to taste beauty or cease to live. When she felt her own beauty fading and found it more and more difficult to hold on to the beauty of the opposite sex and to have it near her, she took a radical step. She launched herself into the kind of world where any woman is in danger of her life just so she could grasp another scrap of 'brown flesh' and the illusion of being desired. No one knew who her murderer was. But we do know the reason for her journey – she revealed it in her letters.[1]

This longing for beauty imposes a kind of tyranny on women in particular, but is there any way of breaking this tyranny without denying the 'power of beauty'? Can we tolerate its rarity and fading without fear or madness? Is it possible to do away with the dictates of attractiveness without repressing our regret at the transience of youth? Is it not regret which should fill the space left by the illusion of beauty as something available to all? In olden times people had religion to help them cope with the fact that not all their earthly wishes came true. We have only our democracy. That is really the only thing we have to hold on to. This might sound confusing, as I have just explained façade aesthetics as being a result of consumer democracy. But there is still the idea of political democracy. I think we should remember the original political promises behind democracy since these are still nowhere near being fulfilled, and we should refuse to tolerate the 'over-fulfilment' of the cultural/consumerist promises, for the substance of these promises has long since been perverted. But what does that mean in effect? Façade aesthetics and the dictates of attractiveness are products of consumer democracy, that much is clear.

Although consumer democracy certainly provides some measure of real satisfaction, it is still like a surrogate, a kind of placebo: it is designed to help people cope with the fact that political democracy has remained incomplete. The populace still does not get the chance to participate in political decision-making which it promised. This is particularly true for women. They are furthest removed from being able to influence politics *and* it is they who can apparently be distracted most effectively by consumerism. Yet it is they who would have particularly good reason to point out the promises which have not been kept. The women's movement's commitment to promote real equality between the sexes is a continuation of the work started by the democratic political parties who downed tools after obtaining the vote for women more than half a century ago.

As women and men take a more active role in running their own lives and in political decision-making and as they communicate socially in a wider variety of fields, so private consumption will become less important. For private consumption is served by malignant consumer democracy and involves the consumption of illusions of attractiveness. It sounds rather grand, but it is true – only by perfecting *political democracy* can we escape from the impasse we have been driven into by the acceleration of consumer democracy. Only then would our lives have any 'point' again. Philosophers are not the only ones searching in the dark for this 'point' and it is mainly because this 'point' is missing that we dare not see our death coming. We dare not receive its harbingers, the decay of our bodies and our fine features, without setting a whole ritual of denial and aestheticization into motion. It is no accident that it was in the fifties, the heyday of the consumerist feminine mystique, when Americans made a perverse cult out of putting make-up and smart clothes on *the dead*.

Certainly, the time-span of political processes (such as political democratization) seems inadequate for the dimensions of a problem such as the aesthetics of sexual attraction. So let us consider whether changes could be made that are more within the range of our personal capabilities. What about 'democratizing' sexual existence? *Men* ought to begin to take a serious view of their *own* sexual existence, perhaps with women's encouragement. When I say sexual existence, I mean their role as sex objects for women as well as their role as fathers, particularly to babies. Most men are not particularly well versed in the art of eroticism and there are only very few who dare to get involved with their offspring. The sexual existence as such seems to count for little socially and seems to be something for women only. In fact, any sexual role (in this case being active within one's sexual existence) is *reciprocal* in arrangement: it is an injustice in itself to say that women sometimes play out their role with an imaginary partner.

As far as the aesthetics of sexual attraction are concerned, reciprocity of 'sexual existence roles', that is with men 'joining in', would undoubtedly serve as a kind of liberation from elements of domination and submission. Both sexes would be looking and both sexes would be presenting themselves for inspection. The ideal of beauty would be bisexual. Attractiveness would no longer be synonymous with femininity and femininity would no longer be synonymous with efforts to be attractive. Instead, men could find out what it is like to show oneself off (homosexual men already know) and women could find out what it is like to dictate what constitutes beauty and to be onlookers. Between subject and object, between onlooker and object, between those enjoying the spectacle and those providing it, the bounds of gender would disappear.

I realize that this Utopia does not sound likely to become reality in the near future. But I think it is more realistic than the total boycott of accepted forms of beauty which the women's movement is offering as basically the only solution. It is impossible to maintain this kind of boycott because the need we all have to be refreshed by the sight of someone beautiful is too deeply lodged within us, both men and women. Women would probably get further ahead in their emancipation if they made an effort to satisfy this need by expecting to find beauty among the opposite sex instead of always referring the need for beauty to their own bodies and understanding it as an encouragement to themselves to be beautiful. And men would gain a great deal if they took a lesson from Narcissus. But before they jump into the lake, they should go and show themselves to women. They are probably held back by fear of how they will be judged, but it could be that this fear is unjustified. We do not know what that judgement would be because it would be the first time in history that such a judgement had been made. I suspect that even Helen of Troy, if she had to choose between three adorned gods, would select the one who promised her Paris, the most beautiful young man in all Greece.

Notes

1   Maryse Holder, *Give sorrow words: Maryse Holder's letters from Mexico*, New York, Grove Press, 1979.

5

The Lost Eroticism of the Breasts

Some time ago, the weekly magazine *Der Spiegel* offered a review of the new feminist press. It gave a brief exposition of the questions most often discussed, and noted, quoting the magazine *Courage*, that there were some '. . . edifying comments about breastfeeding' to be found there.

I am familiar with the issue of *Courage* in question. It appeared in February 1978. It contains several articles about breastfeeding – they are all interesting, but not one of them is edifying. As I read the *Der Spiegel* article I wondered what had moved the editor to use the word 'edifying', despite the fact that the contents of the texts he was reporting were rather depressing.

It must have been association of ideas. That *Der Spiegel* editor had probably not read the articles about breastfeeding himself. He had probably just taken in the headlines and the main points, skimmed over a bit here and there and then, when he decided to include the question of breastfeeding in his report, he probably described it in the only way he thought possible – surely any sort of comment about breastfeeding would be edifying?

The image of the nursing mother is like a Victorian print. A woman with plaits and a lot of petticoats, a wide frill on the open neck of her dress and a double chin. Her rosy-faced baby sleeps at her breast and at her feet there is a yawning cat. Apple blossom can be seen waving through the window. Very edifying.

As far as social awareness of individuals' sexuality is concerned – awareness of their instincts and of their bodies as the bearers and instruments of those instincts – our century may one day be called the 'Freudian' century. Sexuality was and is 'taken seriously' in a way unknown before. It is seen to be the source of every kind of individual conflict, fear and suffering. It became the subject of enlightenment and as such it became something medical which could be 'understood'. Yet at the same time, it was allowed to enjoy its full rights. Thanks to the women's movement, we now know that this is only partly true for women and their instincts. In their case, there is still some enlightenment to come (some sort of enlighten-ment which makes domestication more difficult).

Breastfeeding is a partial expression of female sexuality and yet there is no awareness or understanding of it today, no culture attached to it and not even an inkling of its rank as a sexual potentiality. Needless to say, the patriarchy is to blame for this exclusion, because, after all, in its egocentricity it *had* to ignore this partial expression of human sexuality. I find it more surprising that even the history of the female species formulated by women themselves, however fragmentary, maintains a seldom-interrupted silence over this special sexual experience. We frequently describe our relative lack of history and past dependence as expropriation. Women had their sexual self-confidence, their active role and their pleasure expropriated. They were impoverished. Despite the impoverishment which women were forced to endure as sexual beings in the nineteenth century and long into the twentieth, as lovers, as women who slept with men (or with women), they could still enjoy some last scraps, fragments, of subjectivity. At least for some classes of women such as the 'female Bohème' in the developing cities, sexual potency was permissible: they were allowed a life of their own to search for pleasure. But this life was still limited to the sex act, coitus and the way to it. Anything which may have followed was reproduction and not sexuality, it was burden, pain, duty which, at best, were dealt with willingly. The most inventive female lovers, or those who were particularly favoured by fate and who were unwilling to conform to the bourgeois role, then abstained as completely as possible from 'what followed'. The nineteenth century bourgeoisie – bigotted as it was for the most part – only allowed sexual pleasure if it was aiming towards 'consequences', thereby separating pleasure and sexuality from reproduction. It played one off against the other. Only the male role was the sexual role in the narrower sense and women were only active sexually inasmuch as they accompanied the man in *his* sexual activity. Expropriating women's own sexuality in this way is powerfully reflected in the composition of Freud's libido concept. In her essay 'Die totgesagte Vagina' ('The vagina declared dead'),[2] Renate Schlesier gives very sound grounds for claiming that this concept (or the thing meant by it) is something exclusively *male*. Basically, women were only admitted to the realm of sexuality as guests to be dispatched off towards their 'true' vocation as agents of reproduction. And reproduction was something which happened outside the realm of pleasure, it was God's curse on Eve. Women have to cover the longest part of the road to reproduction with their bodies and yet in this way they became beings existing outside sexuality, outside the delights of orgiastic release, they became asexual mothers, the bearers of unborn children and the bearers of suffering. Breastfeeding too was of course part of this tamed, pleasureless, domesticated world of 'maternal duties'. Thus it came about that carrying children, giving birth and the sexual potentiality of breastfeeding were wholly expropriated from women.

'Wholly' does not mean that individuals do not still realize this potentiality, despite everything. What I am interested in is the social and cultural realization of this potentiality. This was inevitably lacking as long as women were excluded from any theoretical or practical treatment of the sexuality question. Moreover, in view of the quite special, mutually pleasurable contact between bodies which is or may be experienced by new-born babies and their mothers, women ought to put forward the views of two people, since babies cannot speak, according to 'official' or socially accepted and tolerable interpretations. It was impossible for women in particular to speak for two people, because they were used to *letting men speak* and they had first to wear away a thick layer of projections before they were able to speak for themselves. But can we talk about 'self' at all in this context? After all, in sexuality and the cultural expressions of it, what we are always dealing with are *relationships* between two people. The incest-taboo was enough to exclude new-born children from the reckoning, let alone the prevalent restrictions existing as the consequences of the male sexual role. In the course of reproduction, men are present at most as spectators and so, since children cannot be considered as the originators of a relationship, women appear to

be *alone*, devoid of a relationship, left to face the months of
'expecting' and forced to see it through. Looking at it logically,
sexuality was out of the question because sexuality always implies
the presence of a *second party*.

The women's movement has since changed the situation not so
much by looking for ways to articulate the pleasure experienced
during reproduction as by having babies. There was and is a body
of feminist opinion in favour of having children, in other words a
practical critique of what Simone de Beauvoir proposed. More and
more women have learnt how to work their way out of man's
shadow. Some do without male companionship in life and some
'educate' their boyfriends or husbands to share those unspeakable
'household chores' which were considered feminine for so long.
Those same women now want to know what it feels like to have a
baby. The new women's movement never got worked up about
theory but was always pragmatic in the best sense and, true to this
temperament, women are increasing their experience and widening
their knowledge by experimentation. Feminists are carrying babies,
giving birth to them and breastfeeding them. The 'second parties'
in a new sexual experience, hesitantly permitted and undertaken,
are unborn and new-born babies. Men are also involved – but as
fathers, as part of a *ménage à trois*. The modern *couple* is made up of
woman and child (or, less often, man and child), a couple in
pursuit of pleasure, a couple who make love. One of the first people
to state this explicitly was a man – but what does it matter: he is
entirely moulded by his profession, formerly a classic female
profession; he is an obstetrician. Frédéric Leboyer, the famous
French gynaecologist is quite unabashed in his book *Birth without
Violence* when he says that a new-born child is looking for a *lover*. But
not (only) in the spiritual or emotional sense, as is the general
requirement after all, but in the physical sense. The hands which
receive the baby must speak the language of 'internal organs',
writes Leboyer. They must rhythmically caress it, raise it, lower it,
squeeze it and release it in such a way that it is reminded of the
soothing, stimulating massage it received in the uterus before birth.

'But wait a minute' people will say, 'surely that constitutes a
physical act of love with a child.' Of course it does. What else does
the new-born child ask for and what else can adults give it?

When I read this famous book, I was greatly impressed by the sensitivity with which Leboyer guessed what a baby just a few minutes old is asking for with its mouth opening to suckle, its body searching in a state of shock and its heart beating wildly: a physical act of love. I kept staring at these words 'physical act of love'. I must add that I was pregnant when I first read Leboyer's book and I was not content with expecting my baby in the way which our culture offers or prescribes for pregnant women: 'building the nest' as it were (preparing the nursery, going to antenatal classes, and experiencing a general feeling of well-being). With the 'physical act of love' Leboyer put a name to a latent, yet pressing desire. The preparations for the baby allowed by the world around me and the conformity within myself – building the nest and feeling quiet joy – now seemed to me at best, edifying. It all took on secondary importance. The idea of a 'physical act of love' was what fitted in with the expectancy which my body had long been expressing. I did not want edification, but something 'more serious', something which was not so easy to grasp or subdue by conscious or rational thought, something more *risqué*, something closer to ecstasy than mere joy. Leboyer's suggestive language had convinced me that once the child was born it would be open to this 'ecstatic experience' – and now I could admit to myself that I wanted the same thing. My 'hope' grew more intense. Instead of 'responsibility' I had a sense of expectation, expectation of a rendezvous which made my heart race.

At this point I left Leboyer behind. For him, women in childbirth are too wracked with pain, too stupid and too clumsy to carry out the 'physical act of love' – that is Leboyer's mistake. An excellent mistake it was though, for it enabled him to take a radical stand on the side of the child and thus come to a greater understanding. It was an understandable mistake because he himself wanted to take part in such an act. It is a mistake which is also the right one to make, it points us in the right direction by relativizing the role of mothers and the role of gender in the relationship between child and adult and by showing that men too can be 'mothers', in other words, that fathers too are able to carry out this act of love with children. And yet the mistake remains a mistake: the natural 'second party' in the act of love with the new-born child is the mother who has just given birth, with her soft, undulating belly and her erect breasts. However pleasant for the baby the massage given by the obstetrician, the mother's hands could practise the same art when once she is free of the blockade of chemical anaesthetics (indeed so could the father's). Subsequent acts of love (for the child is not satisfied with just one such act postpartum) during the next days, weeks and months, would be the feeding-times – mingling of bodies and bodily fluids, a sexual activity which generates by sustaining life and which gives pleasure, the kind of pleasure we are all familiar with (or would like to be) from coitus. Hardly anyone expects the care given to children by women under the headings of 'reproduction' and 'maternal duties' to include this kind of pleasure.

The uncertain ground I am now moving into by suggesting that there is an element of sexuality present when feeding or mothering a baby is the ground laid by our history. It is not my fault that this physical act of surrender to the child was first robbed of any sexual contact and that it then became a duty, tying women to the home with the threat which any duty implies. In addition, this act of violence was made tolerable by surrounding it with an idyllic view of motherhood to which women subscribed by allowing themselves to be portrayed as 'chubby little mums' and by generally identifying with that portrayal. This idyll – this unbearably 'edifying' picture – was only possible because pleasure, 'seriousness', the 'ecstatic feeling' had been abolished beforehand. Does that mean then that we have to give up the whole thing just to get rid of the 'edifying' part?

While I am busy with the manuscript of this essay, friends and acquaintances keep asking me, as they usually do, 'What are you writing about at the moment?' I hesitate. 'About breastfeeding'. 'About what'? 'About nursing a child at the breast. I want to try to . . .'. 'She's finally turned broody' they think, reacting as the *Der Spiegel* editor did. He had no time for edifying signs. But it is not only his good taste which prevented him from taking an interest in breastfeeding. He suspected something politically reprehensible. How could mother and child be dealt with in terms of nature? Many feminists fear this question as he did. Haven't we been through this before? And didn't it always lead to confinement and enslavement for women? To wit, the *Mutterkreuz*:[3] under the Nazis breastfeeding was obligatory. Again and again women have been driven back to motherhood with references to their *nature*, which demanded necessarily that they have babies and nurse them at the breast. The only consolation for having their prospects limited in this way was a fictitious idyll of motherhood . . .

That is all true, I admit. But it is no reason for *not* making an issue out of the role of sexuality in reproduction, the 'serious' side of childbirth and feeding. The 'edifying' view, and the obligation which goes with it, the idyll and the blackmail about nature, all combine to make a wall of collective falsehood. This wall stands between us, i.e. the women who say 'We want everything' and a state of affairs where we ourselves and the general public are willing to allow the 'serious' side of sexual interaction between mother and new-born child to be experienced and debated. It is like a wall which must be torn down. As long as progressive men continue to shy away from signs of 'edification' when they hear mention of the breastfeeding question and as long as radical feminists do the same, picking up the smell of kitchens and nappies, the wall will remain in place and with it, a piece of false reality. We do not need either the idyll or the obligation any more today. Yet these still go to make up the composite of associations and conditions of real, practical and mental behaviour.

No, we have not yet been through this. Women were placed under obligation to serve the interests of reproduction *without* experiencing pleasure, without experiencing the 'serious' physical sensations of reproduction which are difficult to achieve, yet which can be cultivated. Reproduction was 'God's curse on Eve', nothing but pain, deprivation and deception.

During the Nazi period, mothers had to breastfeed at regular times of the day to ensure good nourishment. There was no question of experiencing pleasure. Instead it was much more important to bring up the child to be robust and accustomed to a fixed routine. A child that did not complete the 'physical act of love' in the prescribed period of time was bullied into doing so. Women were deprived of any hint of physical satisfaction by having to undergo tests to establish how much milk they produced and so on. Just as the Catholic Church bound up sex with conception, 'allowing' only the men's heterosexual orgasm (yet thereby restricting it, i.e. 'castrating' it), so breastfeeding was bound up with nutrition, a way of ensuring that the baby 'thrived', thus effectively removing the delights of the 'physical act of love' from the mother's fragile sexual potentiality.

Apart from the most recent tendencies to the contrary in the women's movement, the situation has remained the same ever since. According to modern, medically inspired sex-education books, breastfeeding means relieving the child's cries of hunger by offering sustenance from the breast. Breastfeeding equals appeasing hunger. Yet I say breastfeeding means satisfying the child's need (and the mother's) to become one again with another body in a 'physical act of love'. The fact that nourishment is given and taken during this act is of secondary importance for our purpose, just as the possibility of conception is of secondary importance for the 'serious' side of enlightened discourse on sexuality and the coital act of love. Since today it is no longer a problem to rear babies on artificial food, we can quite happily forget the 'duty' which breastfeeding was always made out to be for women. We are now able (speaking theoretically and analytically) to make a distinction between the feeding function and the latent love function which is to be rediscovered. This distinction which, of course, does not exist in practice, must be clear in our minds if we want to escape from the uncertain ground mentioned above. Enlightened men *and* emancipated women want to trick us into returning there, that is, those who cannot tolerate the word 'breastfeeding' because they associate it either with edification or with pressure and duty. It is easy to see the analogy to the liberation of sex from the biological, generative function. Today there are no longer any (serious) 'biological' reasons for a mother to nurse her child at the breast. For *precisely this reason* minorities in the women's movement were able to find their way back to breastfeeding, but to breastfeeding as a source of pleasure and thereby a move towards female emancipation.

Fair enough, but what can we really say about the question of '*faire l'amour*' by breastfeeding except that women and babies have been robbed of an experience which it is right and worthwhile to win back? Well, I think this question offers a particularly good opportunity to talk about *nature* (body, instinct, desire) without the risk of being caught up at the very outset in the complicated reciprocities and reflections of reflections involved in defining the sexes. In this case, our starting point is sexuality (the body), and we are only concerned with the sex of one partner because we can disregard the sex of the 'other' party, the child.

First of all the reluctance to identify women with their 'nature' is justified historically in a manner of speaking. Nevertheless, nature (body, instinct, desire) can always be seen as a *point de résistance* against any kind of socialization which brings conformity or subordination. But for women this liberating perspective also has its drawback.

For too long the female body had been the very cage into which the whole sex had been forced. This body was fertile and fertility became the idyllized limit of women's opportunities (and even the idyll, this weak sticky consolation, was only granted to the higher social classes). But fertility is never just 'fertility alone', there is no pure biology in the socialized world. Instead, it is society itself which reduces things to a biological level, something which has been perpetrated during our history, not as a result of nature itself. Real (human, female) nature has disappeared, dispersed among the historical transformations (the forms of coexistence).

But even though women have been, and still are, cheated by false invocation of their nature, there can be no liberation which is not based on their nature. Nature in this case would not be 'pure' (i.e. nature *alone*) but nature experienced as a woman's own, felt, defined and *transcended* by the woman herself. Nature taken as a pretext for suppression is always flawed – indeed it becomes 'impure', crippled. But that means that we must have recourse to nature as we work to escape from suppression, and I don't mean an unflawed kind of nature, but one which may be socialized in a different, beneficial way. The fact that a huge number of women in industrialized parts of the world have lost the natural eroticism of their breasts, eroticism directed towards a child – is a sign of flawed nature. I call this eroticism 'natural' because I believe it forms a part of female instinctual potentiality which comes into the world with female individuals, being inherent in their bodies. But it is only a potential phenomenon. The question will always be whether the social climate is favourable enough to incubate a kind of physical potentiality and fuse it into reality. As far as women's breasts are concerned, there has been a polar climate in the upper classes since the beginning of modern times. Only today are changes taking place. The potentialities are suddenly being felt and defined – and now the social imagination can also look for ways of *developing* them.

So 'liberation on the basis of nature' would mean *developing* the body's inherent potentialities. This development would once again be a social act, thereby removed from the realms of a fictitious 'pure' nature. Only when it is (socially) developed is the biological potentiality 'mature' and real. We could also say that nature can only be realized through society. And yet what has then *become real* is no longer 'nature', but shape, form, a particular condition of life. In other words, culture. Summing up, what women would have to bring about would be a cultivation of the eroticism of the breasts and of breastfeeding. By that I don't mean adequate feeding of a baby (which, happily, coincides with it but which should not be of paramount importance). What I mean is the art of love, the expression of female sensuality, intermingling of bodies, or even ecstasy.

How this cultivation should be achieved I dare not say yet; but that this cultivation has a basis in nature we can demonstrate once more by an analogy:

> The parallel between breastfeeding in particular and the hetero-sexual sex act is superficially more obvious than the actual similarities in sensation and arousal would suggest. The tip of the breast, a highly sensitive, erectile organ pushes its way into the baby's warm and moist oral cavity. While the lips, jaws and gums close around the organ, massaging it in a rhythmic sucking motion, it discharges its special juice into the child's deeper oesophageal region. But in this case there is no steep pattern of pleasure with a clearly marked climax and sudden decrease, but instead a flat pattern with one or two moderate eruptions, for instance when the milk suddenly bursts forth after the first minutes of hesitant flow, as if it had taken a while to find its way.[4]

The similarity between the two forms of 'love' seems to me great enough to allow us to explain how one form may be cultivated by looking at how the other is cultivated. How could the analogy continue (an analogy which is only intended to serve as a help to the mind and imagination)? Some women experience an aching pain below the solar plexus when separated from the baby they are suckling. This is the kind of pain normally felt only by loving couples when they are forced to be apart. Women experience the welling of their white mammary fluid with the same pride with which a boy fingers his semen: life-giving (and sustaining) material which finds its pleasure-tinged way into another body. I do not believe at all that these analogies are so lame. What is lame is reality. Because in reality it is indeed only 'some women' who feel this way. Perhaps I should say *few* women. Many mothers are disgusted by their milk, they do not like it when it leaks out between feeding-times and makes their skin wet. They feel shocked at their erect breasts. They react like a monk expiating a forbidden ejaculation by castigating himself. They resist the eroticism of their breasts and ask for treatment so they can relax. Without practice or relevant knowledge, sex always hovers between pleasure and disgust and succumbs to the latter if there is no cultivation, no form of refinement, rite, or language to ratify and organize it.

Even during periods when breastfeeding was 'in favour' – most recently in our own century – there has not been the right climate for developing fully the sensuality which centres on the breasts. As the nineteenth century moved into the twentieth, the ability to breastfeed became something scientific with the growth of medicine and pedagogy, so that the phenomenon was under the control of (male) experts and officials instead of being subject to the feelings of women and children. It was directed into a narrow, straightened channel instead of being left to run its course, driven along by currents of pleasure. It did not have to be a wild, undefined course – I do not mean that alternative ('raw' nature) – but it could have been cultivated and turned into an art.

In cultivating an instinct (or part of an instinct), developing a physical potentiality (which aims at pleasure), it is possible to stay well away from the (raw) natural form and to refine it in the most diverse ways. We know for instance that many, and perhaps all, highly developed civilizations recognize an *ars amandi*, an art of love, in which reproduction is no longer important. Instead, the emphasis is on the most diverse follies, games, role reversals – refined forms of sex (which are now marginalized as 'perversions' or homosexuality in our underdeveloped erotic culture, because sex has become so clinical). Of course, these refined forms of sex were strictly reserved for those who lived in luxury at the top of the social heap. And yet there is another reservation. Since all great civilizations in recent history had a patriarchal structure, the female body was not cultivated. When I say this, I am thinking about the potential pleasure found *within* reproduction (birth, breastfeeding) which was being noticed continually, but which has never been completely cultivated and refined. Even the 'perversions' and gender-swapping games connected with this potential pleasure, if discovered at all, have been completely forgotten in our civilization (a sign of a general failure to cultivate pleasure in reproduction). Is anyone today aware of the fact that even the male breast can produce milk if it is stimulated enough by a baby's mouth (not enough milk to feed the baby, but enough to intensify the pleasure exchange)? Would any man think of putting a newborn child under his shirt before feeding it, and letting it suck on his nose or his tongue when it has eaten enough but still wants to suck? There will be many male readers who will balk at this – but that is the same prejudice which Eskimos show when they find out that people of other cultures kiss with their lips.

A cultivated eroticism of the breasts could change our everyday life. I will keep to my analogy because it is the only way to bridge the gap in my imagination. Imagine a couple – to make it simpler, a newly married couple, because the social consensus is particularly broadminded in such a case. A couple on their honeymoon enjoy all the privileges left for situations beyond the normality of everyday life. Everyone heeds the 'Do not disturb' sign on the hotel room door, everyone wishes the couple all the best, leaves them in peace, drinks toasts to them, looks fondly upon them and gives them gifts. In short, there is a kind of social respect for (legalized) love. There is now also a certain respect, albeit less widespread, for free love. If the pleasure in reproduction were cultivated, women with children at their breasts would also deserve and win this kind of respect or freedom from restrictions. Of course, it would be shown in a different way, for the analogy is only an analogy and many details would be quite new. But even so, there would be a shift in the scale of priorities governing our daily lives: there would be space and time for the sensual qualities of pregnancy, birth and feeding to come through. How else should children grow up? If babies had a language and a script we would have been in possession long ago of a manual of polished love techniques for use between adults and babies. Clinical care and pedagogic concern would be cast onto the rubbish-tip of civilization, and with them that cheap edification which a critical mind rejects quite rightly. What – by the way – that editor from *Der Spiegel* did not notice or was unable to notice, was that the first feminist essays on breastfeeding were concerned precisely with dismantling this idyll, the 'edifying' side, and as well as criticizing the idyll, they expressed an inkling of the sensuous potential which had been submerged.

Of course, there are feminists who associate breastfeeding with 'edification' (or coercion) in the same way. They want nothing (or the least possible) to do with motherhood because they believe that everything connected with reproduction pushes women further into a ghetto – even if it is an 'emancipated' ghetto – simply because only women can have babies. What narrow-mindedness! Things are not like that, or they do not have to be. To put it very boldly, men can have babies too – at least as far as the sensual and erotic part of the process is concerned. Use can be made of my analogy again here – but I leave that to the imagination of the reader. In the context of this essay, it is a question of how far there has developed an *ars amandi* with respect to new-born babies, how far men are prepared to go as 'mothers', or more precisely, as fathers in eroticism. This is where I see men playing a part in caring for babies at any rate. We women can and must put pressure on men, force them to take on some of the duties involved in looking after children. It is essential that these duties are shared if women are to win equality in any other field. But we can also *win over* the men by offering them a share in pleasure. Babies are looking for food and comfort from the breast – and they could get comfort just as well from the fine and sensitive breasts of men.

One more thing – it is very important to me to include a potentiality like breastfeeding under the term 'sexuality' because the ability to *satiate* (or fulfil, if you prefer a grander term) and the subsequent temporary *distance* from the love object, the whole cycle of sensation and activity, is a quite particular characteristic of sexual expression and activity and I would be so pleased to see it as an integral part of the early relationship between mother and child. I believe that mothers who desired their children and were able to satiate ('feed') themselves on their children will find it easier to let go of them and the children will also find the separation easier to bear. Unlikely as it may sound, the eroticism of the breasts would also have the function of *loosening* the all too close ties between mother and child.

Notes

1 The new West German feminist press includes a number of small journals or newspapers which are mainly of local importance. But there are three names which are known nationally: *Emma*; *Courage* (monthly journal from Berlin); and *Die schwarze Botin* (an academic journal). [Ed.]

2 In Brigitte Wartmann (ed.), *Weiblich-Männlich: Kulturgeschichtliche Spuren einer verdrängten Weiblichkeit*, Berlin, Ästhetik und Kommunikation Verlag, 1980.

3 *Mutterkreuz* was a Nazi medal awarded to mothers who had four or more children [Ed.].

4 Barbara Sichtermann, *Leben mit einem Neugeborenen. Ein Buch über das erste halbe Jahr*, Frankfurt, Fischer Taschenbuch, 1981, p. 76.

6

'Cut With a Knife of Ivory'

The Difficulties Women have Forming
Objects and the Consequences of this for Love

One of the first feminist songs of the early seventies ended with the belligerent chorus:

> United we are stronger
> Objects in bed no longer
> Women, throw off your bonds.

The first line was an older watchword which had already featured in a Berlin demonstration in 1969, if I remember correctly. That was on May Day at a time when the word 'feminism' was still rare. The demonstration was not specifically to do with women's problems, yet a block of women demonstrated on their 'own account'. What appeared two years later as the new mass women's movement had its diverse but significant precursors.

The words of that early protest song were a very accurate reflection of the essence of the feminist revolt: what they were concerned with was bringing an end to their object status – not only in bed, but in economic life too. The song covered everything: 'In adverts we're just Barbie dolls' and 'We're the low-paid workers', but it was 'Objects in bed no longer' which recurred again and again in the chorus. It was this kind of object status which had to go, above all else.

Putting an end to object status would be another way of describing the women's revolt (another way of describing any revolt). The implications of this are important. Anyone who is no longer prepared to be an object (of whatever) must first dethrone a subject who has forced him/her to assume a certain role. He/she must then set him/herself up, not necessarily in exactly the same position, but he/she must assume subject status, at least changing the status quo to start with. Anyone who is no longer prepared to be an object shuns the treatment, degradation, manipulation, definition etc. meted out by another. He or she breaks out of a relationship which – let us be cautious – was infected with signs of domination and submission and which bore the marks of coercion in some way. If the break-out is successful, the former object is then 'free'. That does not yet determine how things will develop subsequently. The relationship may change round (like a wrestling match where attacker and defender are roles in which the two participants alternate) or it may just dissolve: once liberated, woman leaves her one-time oppressor and goes away. Period.

It is clear that all relationships between people and between people and things can be construed in terms of subject and object, even those where submission and domination are present only in a very sublimated way. My formalized description of 'putting an end to object status' therefore has its weaknesses because it fits too many cases. But it may serve to elucidate if we use its simplicity to formulate a question which will perhaps take us further, and if we keep in mind that the objects in question are quite specific historically. We are talking about objects in bed – the kind of object status which contributed to the start of the feminist movement, and which was also included in the idea of 'bonds'. 'We've got to get out of this place' the women said looking at the hearts, beds, houses but also the words, lines and vows of their men. 'These places' had become prisons for them. They moved out and were then 'free'.

Much has already been said about the consequences of this. The dethroned subjects tried to maintain their position and where they did not succeed, they gave up and quailed. It was the beginning of the period of debate on 'emancipation-afflicted men'. 'Female Utopias – male losses' was one of the headlines. The old subject-object relationship was destroyed (not for the majority but certainly for the feminist avant-garde and its male retinue). In its place there was at first only triumph, grievance, reflection, the emotional or mental absorption of this destruction. But there was no recognizable new constellation of forces.

The question which I would now like to extract from my

formalized description of the revolt is this – how can women, 'liberated objects' as they are, form objects of their own? Are they able to do so? Are they even trying? Are they allowed to? Do they want to? 'Form objects' is another quite abstract expression. But we will let it stand for a while. If we do so we will have a chance of avoiding the question of beds for a time so that we can first be clear on the implications of these questions.

'Forming objects' does not necessarily mean 'forcing into submission', – after all, objects can offer resistance. First and foremost, it means placing oneself in an active relationship with the world. Every curious child makes the world an object for its perception, for its desire to experiment, but it only forces into submission those particles which oblige it anyway. 'Forming objects' would thus seem to mean taking hold, appropriating. But also creating distance in order to observe, evaluate and then turn away: picking out a thing, a person or a variety of persons and things, setting them apart, isolating them and wanting to know what makes them tick, and then at some time passing on to something else. It would mean seizing the object, holding it, doing something with it, letting it go, looking at it, judging it: a process during which both parts, subject and object, may change.

As far as forming objects in the social world is concerned, women are handicapped by a historical weakness. Even after centuries they have scarcely learnt how to do it. How then can they be expected to be capable of it now, in this age of emancipation, just like that? Forming objects – seizing and viewing parts of the world around us, or more generally, taking an active role by bringing something into one's power – is not something which comes naturally to human beings. It is a potentiality which requires encouragement and some tradition behind it; incentive and history; precedent and after-effect. Women lack these stimuli. They must first produce them from within themselves. There are certainly plenty of exceptions to this – that is, women who were able to objectivize from scratch as it were, and this is something which women are now concerned with reconstructing. But for the majority it is true to say that they have first to produce the very conditions for their emancipation, an ability to form objects which is fundamental to any step they may take. This is an enormous task.

> Feminism urges women to bring matter into their power. It calls on
> them saying: we must assail history, philosophy and science, we
> must get our teeth into logic and dialectics, capture art which the
> male spirit has set up over the centuries drawing nourishment like a
> vampire from the fettered female ego.[1]

So says a feminist text from the start of things eight years ago. It
makes me think of another word: aggressiveness. This is what
women must learn 'from scratch', they must develop it and show it
as a feeling, a movement, an action. The new women's movement
was aggressive from the start, aggressive in its stance and in its way
of expressing itself, but its aggression was also a polemical talent.
The movement found the right tone from the first moment. It was
that which made it so fearsome and that which got it publicity

Of course, all through history women have possessed their 'own'
objects: they had children who also tied them down, they had
washing to do which piled up around them, and they had men, who
were close to their hearts, but on whom they were always
dependent. Caring for things is also a form of objectivization, and it
can also be consolidated into a way of bringing something into your
power, which has certainly happened many times. But this form of
objectivization has the disadvantage that it never isolates the object
enough. It never removes it from its context, and there is not
enough distance between subject and object for the subject to be
able to abandon the object, temporarily or permanently. If object
formation is to be seen as a kind of sovereign appropriation which
can and will be discontinued subsequently, then the subject must
be able to abandon the object whenever it wants to.

In view of women's 'historical weakness' I would regard it as
perfidy to devote a whole section to men's superior capabilities in
'isolating objects' as a biological and gender-specific difference. I
objectivize any book saying that kind of thing to such an extent that
I hurl it out of the window. Such theories still abound even among
progressive authors who serve the cause of emancipation but who
want to remain 'realistic' at the same time.

As a sex, we have become weak at forming objects, but that is the
legacy of history. It will not be so much longer: we will bring about
a new form of objectivization, by creating a new order of things. For

the moment there are many problem areas remaining as a consequence of our weakness, as we have been able to define and objectivize this weakness since we left object status behind. Our weakness and the beginning of the end of that weakness, is what makes our situation so difficult.

What situation? Let us now leave aside formalizations and generalizations again. They have helped thus far, but continuing to use them would make my arguments too vague. The situation in question is that of the sexes, of the relationship between them. Now we are getting back to the question of object status in bed.

Some years ago, around the time when women were being urged to assail art and science, I read a critique of that early feminist song (or perhaps of something else where men were accused of being cold objectivizers in bed). It went something like this: 'If women feel like objects in bed, it is their own fault. Why do they sleep with men they do not desire?'

Unfortunately I have forgotten who wrote this – I only know it was a *woman*. It is obvious that this woman was making the same mistake as the progressive biologist who claimed that the ability to isolate objects was distributed unevenly between the sexes at a genetic level. She disregarded the 'historical weakness,' or better, the historical nature of our weakness (at forming objects). Desiring means objectivizing and objectivizing in a quite radical way. Can women overcome an age-old weakness overnight?

The writer in question would probably reply at this point 'Are you claiming that women are unable to feel desire?' I would have to say 'No, but . . .'. Female desire is a broken, fragmentary, distorted, deformed instinct. Even while it is still only searching for its object it is inhibited, diverted, forced to keep silent or move on. Not only, as I said, because women have subjective difficulties in forming objects, but mainly because the potential objects put up stiff opposition to being seized, sometimes even just ignoring the attempt which is made to seize them. Women's inability to form objects is not just a historically conditioned atrophy which came about because women never had the chance to learn how to do it. It is a constantly present, constantly reinflicted mutilation, because the potential objects resist isolation, they resist seizure, evaluation and rejection. They do this almost as a reflex action, and this behaviour is legitimized by a complete superstructure of norms, morals, customs and – if I may put it like this – social climates. It is a process which happens without those involved knowing how negatively it affects women's (already limited) ability to form objects.

If what I say about men here is correct, the consequence is twofold. Firstly, men are not prepared (or not able) to let themselves be desired. Secondly, women must either reconstruct their ability to desire or redirect it. Taking the last point first: it seems to me that both things happen. Female desire 'lacks confidence', it is ineffectual, it is unable to anticipate or go further afield, and it is not allowed to rear its head. For this reason it is not possible for it to become sophisticated or to be concentrated. After all, it can only grow and develop on the basis of an object. If the object resists being an object and woman's hold on it grows faint-hearted, her fantasies will remain childish and bound up in clichés. Any elements of desire left are turned in on the subject and revolve around her own ego. The so-called erotic women who have love on their minds and are pursued by men have in many cases learnt simply to concentrate their libidinal energies on themselves. Female narcissism in this form is a makeshift solution.

Back to the first point: are men really not prepared to let themselves be desired? They may well want to, but they are seldom able to. This is one area in which men have learnt no better even after centuries. In the relationship between the sexes, oppression always comes back as self-oppression, not because the object of oppression fights back, but because of the dialectic involved. Men cannot suddenly let themselves be made into objects, just as women cannot suddenly know how to form objects. This is men's historical weakness and perhaps it is now clear at last just how complex and intertwined are the bonds which women have been singing about for ten years.

The women who protested did not suggest that women now had to form objects and take on subject status in bed. They did not try to reverse the relationship. This is an important point. Instead, many women broke off their relationships with men and turned to other women if they felt the impulse and desire to form sexual objects. Only in this situation, among equals, did it seem possible to overcome the historical weakness gradually. Verena Stephan's successful novel *Shedding*, written in 1975, is an account of this period.[2] Female desire which wanted to express itself fully and thereby become a true female desire, ignored men as a systematic matter of course. It was as if men were no longer considered to be sexual beings because they had failed at being objects and had gone too far as objectifiers.

I am not talking about individual women or couples now. After all, what do I know about them? I am talking about the discussion among feminists (and other interested and progressive parties) which had now become public. Women made hardly any attempt to form objects in sexuality apart from lesbian relationships.

In that respect it is remarkable that in other areas – politics, art, science and advertizing – women made up for lost time in no uncertain terms, as if this was their 'training' in object formation. The call to women in 1974 'We must assail . . .' sounded so euphorically aggressive because women had long been preparing to conquer the domains which had been closed to them and they could be held back no longer. Women objectified townscapes with their cameras, objectified the history of women's oppression (until then suppressed) by doing research, objectified parliaments and law courts by handing in petitions and objectified public debate with the explosive concept of 'feminism'. They claimed the street, television and many other platforms for themselves. People were forced to listen. Laws had to be rewritten. Women had to be taken seriously, included in the reckoning. Everywhere women were seizing, appropriating, reshaping. Small triumphs in terms of world history, but large strides away from their historical weakness.

Yet in bed it was apparently enough to have rid themselves of object status, they did not begin to objectify men, they just broke away from them.

Do not misunderstand me here, of course there were still couples. It may also be that the younger generation feel capable of doing things which I have no idea about – I cannot speak for them. Yet at that time (and still today) it seemed that women were merely aware that a problem existed, and this awareness seemed to be a permanent disorder which came between the partners in a sexual relationship, as if there was no real prospect of true innovation in the relationship, no strategic solution. Excuse the military expression, but if anything is bad it is not the fact that I use it here but the fact that it fits the situation.

In the final analysis, women will just have to take the plunge and objectify in sexuality too if they are to be truly emancipated. (And the men who are dependent on women in these exceptional cases will have to risk letting themselves be objectified.) The revolt advocated an end to object status and a serious attempt by women to form objects of their own, and this general formulation was general in the true sense of the word: there can be no exceptions. United, women may be strong in many respects, but this united front is of limited use in overcoming their historical weakness in their relationship with men (in love relationships or in sexuality). In sexuality, failure to take an interest in the potential object is not only an insult, in a subtle and tacit way it is a recognition of the superiority and unattainability of the object. In other words, we are back to submission.

Sexual liberation in the sixties was concerned with getting people to admit that sexuality actually existed and that it had to be given its rightful place. It was really a move to liberate sexuality itself and less so the sexes within it. Now it is the turn of individuals. The females among them must make the step and begin to form objects, or else it will be back to the old roles in bed. Men also suffer from a historical weakness, but they have an easier time of it: it is more difficult for them to relapse into the old roles because the objects they are used to forming refuse to comply. Since there are many men who would like to serve the women's movement but do not know how, here is a tip: they could be a bit reticent about forming objects (isolating, evaluating, letting go, see above) and thereby make it much more difficult for women to relapse.

Anyone who talks about sexuality and liberation should be aware that they do so with an air of resignation. It may indeed be possible to liberate sexuality – but what of the individuals within it? Sexuality is also a bond after all, and as soon as sexuality is free, we become ensnared in its bonds. Instead of liberating, we should perhaps talk of living within sexuality according to our *own* wishes.

Sexuality has the power to make *us* (women and men) into its object by means of the partner in each case. Someone feeling desire is an object to that desire and therefore also an object to his/her object: this is why men too are familiar with object status in the bedroom. As the (indirect) objects of their own desire, they are nevertheless freer, in the sense that they are living within sexuality according to their own wishes, than women who are not allowed to develop their own feelings of desire and therefore remain dependent on the desire of others. Here lies the inequality of the sexes in matters of love.

I could also say that once you can choose whether you allow yourself to be objectified, it requires courage because it involves a risk. When it is me who acts, when I myself make the choice and form an object, I am far more certain that what happens will be of benefit to me than when I allow something to be done to me (by becoming an object). This vulnerability, this Achilles heel, 'willingness to surrender' as it was probably called in the old vocabulary of love, is what makes pleasure real. If the *whole* body becomes vulnerable (the old female role), then fear overcomes any pleasure, the object becomes a victim. But if there is not even one vulnerable spot, if there is no unprotected area controlled by the other party in love and sex (the old male role), then security overcomes pleasure and pleasure is no longer able to exclude its astonishingly transcendental potentiality. In the meantime there has been a considerable amount of literature written by women about their agonizing experiences in bed with men who were too good at objectifying. Strange that more men have not expressed their disappointment at nights spent with over-passive women. What kind of pleasure can it be that feeds exclusively on its own projections?

Yet on this point there *is* a body of male testimony protesting against not being allowed to be an object, and this is contained in the relatively rich history of male homosexuality. In the field of literature in particular, a verse drama comes to mind, a small decadently enraptured work, *Salome* by Oscar Wilde. Here we have a perfect reversal of roles: it is the woman who forms her object with an unswerving and stirring fervour, monomaniacal in a way only seen before in young heroes serenading their loved ones. And the object in question recoils in horror. True, in the play it is his mission, his religious fervour which causes the prophet Jochanaan to resist objectification by the lustful princess. But we can interpret the play quite happily in a way which relates to the matter dealt with here. The author, a homosexual *enfant terrible* in Victorian England and bourgeois Paris, certainly knew why the subject matter appealed to him.

Salome's hymns to Jochanaan show all the elements of objectification in love: isolation, analysis and – as a way of maintaining the distance between subject and object – aestheticization. The moment she has the prophet in her mind, or better, in her senses, she knows no other man, she isolates him and herself by her desire from the rest of the world. And she splits him up into part objects, taking each of his lures in turn. She sings of his hair, his body, his mouth. 'Thy mouth is like a pomegranate cut with a knife of ivory.' And what is his answer (a man called to higher, better, more serious things) to this onslaught from a powerful, grasping, determining and fixating desire? 'Back, daughter of Sodom!' That is what a man says to a woman who has made him her (love) object. The prophet, who incidentally still makes a feeble attempt to save Salome's soul, has his own religious reasons for rejecting the lustful woman; the wordly man in the street has inherited something of this. He will only really be drawn into the 'Sodom' of sensual pleasure once he allows himself to be objectified, with all the unnerving selection, isolation, and distancing which that implies. He has always managed to avoid being drawn in because women's historical weakness has kept temptation at bay. But what would happen if, having put an end to their object status, women now began to reverse the relationship slowly and gradually?

I do not intend to spend any more time considering what would happen to men in such a case – men take second place in my considerations. I am talking about us women. By objectifying we stand only to gain. So I hope that we will give it a try and learn how to do it.

I must confess to having my own personal reasons for expressing this hope. A protective hand of the goddess Venus has kept me from suppressing my desire completely, and so despite despising men for their pretentions, I am still hopelessly in love with the opposite sex – their prehistoric hairiness, their outdated poses, their angular contours and their 'emancipation-afflicted' grumblings are what make them so captivating and desirable for me. Infatuation? Certainly, but one which teaches me to see things in a different way. Simone de Beauvoir said that love was a trap and women should take care not to get caught in it for the good of their emancipation. She probably meant that captivation which marks the beginning of love between the sexes and, as we all know, colours our judgement. What one-dimensional thinking, how unlike that famous philosopher! That captivation does not just divert attention (in some cases from emancipation), it also concentrates it (on the man) and in this respect it is the most decisive objectifier imaginable. At hardly any other time do we form an *object* in such a concerted way as when we submit to this captivation. In hymnic adoration and the tenderest pursuit, there is after all a strict distance precisely because adoration and pursuit are in a way incongruous, something alien by everyday standards. We isolate, seize, handle the object by desiring it, we do something to it even if it is only in our minds at first. We anticipate its movements, we pursue it and eavesdrop on what it says. We set it loose as a trial. We seize it again, from another side this time. We change it. Why withhold this lesson in object formation from women?

As a woman who has *not* given up forming objects while captivated, I know the snags of the situation. As objectifiers we tend to prescribe roles in a one-sided way. The frenzy of object formation under the spell of love has a dynamism of its own which may serve to curb an inclination towards passivity, towards *being* an object. If I tell a man his mouth is like a pomegranate cut by a knife of ivory then I expect his mouth to say nothing. I expect it to open slightly, but not to utter some flattery which would in any case hardly match up to the image of the pomegranate and the ivory knife. Certainly today I have a historic right to expect this, but if in future women learned how to form objects and men how to be objects, I would have no such right any longer. There would have to be an awareness of how close objectivization is to domination and a balance would have to be struck beyond the level of domination by making the new positions fluid. The prerequisites for pleasure would then be both objectification and being an object – that is, passivity.

Let us imagine that women draw their ivory knife, carefully and unrepentently, and use it to open men's mouths. Is that too aggressive an image? No, it is one which is long overdue from our point of view. Is it a Utopian image? Perhaps not. What is this knife of ivory? Looks, words, the tongue? Those things too: it is the art of objectification while under the spell of love.

Notes

1   *Schwarze Protokolle*, 124, 1974, p. 20. *Schwarze Protokolle* was a political journal which existed from 1972 to 1977. It was directed against the new dogmatism into which some sections of the 1968 students' movement had lapsed. [Ed.]

2   Verena Stefan's novel *Häutungen* (Munich, Frauenoffensive, 1975; translated by Johanna Moore and Beth Weckmüller under the title *Shedding*, London, Women's Press, 1979) and was the first novel to emerge from the new feminist consciousness in West Germany in the seventies. It was both controversial and hugely successful, selling 165,000 copies by 1979. [Ed.]

7

The Knight in Shining Armour
Reflections on a Banal Myth

As girls are growing up, nearly all their dreams to do with love and sexuality and their emotional and physical future contain a *knight in shining armour*. Instead of 'knight' I could have written hero, or Prince Charming for that matter. At some point a shining figure is supposed to burst into the girl's world and transform everything. How are we to treat this ever-present female worldly fantasy, this dream which is apparently susceptible to disillusionment as much as to incorrigible repetition? Should we just laugh about it, reject it as the cliché it is and wake up the dreamers?

Are such dreams really individual dreams? Since they are so common it is questionable whether they are capable of occupying something as singularly personal as a young girl's imagination. But apparently they do. The dream of a knight in shining armour almost merits being called part of the collective imagination, a myth. Nevertheless it is a cliché. In many clichés, mythical messages are preserved or renewed, and the only chance these myths have of surviving in the age of mass production is if they take on an 'industrial' form, if they become clichés. That is because clichés have the power to enhance the authenticity of memories, to adapt them to what has become the consensus of feeling, or 'sympathy', in other words to replace them with a uniform interpretation. They may also do away with the immediacy of experience, muscling in between subject and object so that perception stops at the edge of the cliché and orders the things around it according to the principles of the cliché, not according to the principles of the object in question.

On the other hand, was it not inevitable that the cliché, the common expression, would make the object resemble it, having

long made its mark on the individual object? And how was the
cliché to have come about and remained alive if it had not been a
vehicle for traces of a real collective wish? As far as our subject is
concerned, that means that the quite specific longing of a particular
young girl for a man is distorted or reduced by the knight figure
and yet is apparently invested with a mythical or collective
historical form. At the same time, the man who is longed for, and
perhaps even found, can do nothing but exhibit the attributes of a
knight in shining armour, thus feeding the dream once more. This
is because both parties, the girl and the man, the bride and the
'knight', move in a world whose conventions and symbols prescribe
both emotion and self-expression. It is one of the most stupid
mistakes of subjective literature to assume that dreams, fantasies
and wishes, all those things people note down uncensored in their
diaries, letters or conversations, are somehow more authentic than
the products of the mind which have been processed by thought. In
fact, whether we are old or young, our dreams are one of the *least*
individual expressions of ourselves.

Fair enough. So we can reject the knight dream as a cliché in our
critique, discard it, 'refuse to accept it' – but we can also take it
seriously as being something loaded with the remains of mythical
messages and we can then try to interpret it. We will then find that
it has something to tell us about the relationship and behaviour of
both sexes towards sexuality.

Let us stay with young girls to start with. Their knight in shining
armour dreams come just at the time when they are leaving school
or beginning to work on higher mathematics and the like, so they
have many things on their minds which have very little to do with
medieval romance. Their longings, fantasies and notions of
sexuality stretch out before them like a mysterious oasis in the
desert of pressures and anxieties which must be crossed on the
route to adulthood. It is as if this desert needed to be irrigated with
streams of wildly romantic myths, which may be so trivial and vain
that one is almost led to despair. It is as if during this period which
demands so much rationality, down to earth practicality and
energy, wonders were necessary to make it bearable, even if they
are only five-minute wonders.

The knight figure or the idea of a *romantic love adventure* holds the promise of a *decisive turn* and a *new beginning*. It brings the prospect of a 'sudden leap out of the time continuum' and resurrection in this world. The knight appears, bewitches the beautiful child and is captivated by her – in a flash, in the blink of an eye, one look is enough – he lifts the girl up onto his charger and rides away with her. Nothing is the same as it was before and the future is uncertain. One thing is sure, the parents who weep for their lost daughter no longer matter, the places of her childhood are left behind as the couple exchange their first kisses rocked by the motion of the faithful steed.

A fantasy of leave-taking and departure: but how are the roles cast? What we as feminists do not like about this dream is that any activity is on the man's side: he *comes* riding up, he *lifts* the girl onto the horse, he *rides* away with her. She appears as an object, the booty, perhaps even as a victim, but in any case she is passive. But wait. This *ad hoc* feminist interpretation is not quite accurate. In that sequence of actions – arriving, lifting onto the horse, riding away – the most essential part is missing: the *coup d'oeil*, the moment of falling in love. In this moment when their eyes meet, some form of activity must be present, coming out of the door for instance, with a pitcher of water in her hand. She has to appear in the knight's field of vision, look at him, etc. At the moment when their eyes meet they are both equally active – looking, smiling, whispering; and equally passive – being looked at, listening, etc. Of course, I am assuming now that the girl does in fact fall in love and that she wants to ride away with him.

The second mistake of the *ad hoc* interpretation is that the language of the dream is taken literally. Is the knight really a man – 'the' man? Even in daydreams it is often a good idea to check whether the longing and object of that longing, and then perhaps subject and object again, should not be interchanged before the message will make any sense. When interpreting female rape fantasies the same mistake was made: no actual interpretation was done, commentators seemed to regard the fantasy as if it were a newspaper advertisement and took the content at face value. Needless to say, it was men who put forward this wrong interpretation because it was in their interest to do so. So let us put things right: when women increase their pleasure with fantasies of rape, the violence of the act is merely a cipher for the violence of their own desire. The woman may not necessarily realize that herself and so she may be horrified by what goes through her mind, but the explanation for this is harmless. The woman does not really want violence from a man but she translates the violence of her desires into a common image, the first cliché that fits by combining violence with sexual activity. In exactly the same way, the 'knight in shining armour' seems to me to be nothing more than a cipher for love itself or for 'grown up' physical desires, for sexuality. It is sexuality which is supposed to come and lift the child onto the horse and carry it off. Sexuality is more powerful than the parents' tears and it wipes out the memory of the things of childhood. We could suggest a further interpretative parallel here: the knight may be understood as a projection, that is, sexuality may once again be replaced by the subject itself, or rather supplemented, endowed with attributes originating from the subject -- fierceness (in appearance), tenderness (as he looks at the girl and picks her up), decisiveness (in riding away). These qualities would then be descriptions of the girl's own desires – she herself is fierce in her sexual desires, etc.

If it is really 'permissible' as an interpretation to put sexuality itself in place of the knight (and I believe this interpretation is not only permissible but correct) then feminists can raise no further objections to the good old knight-in-shining-armour dream. Interpreting it my way, it is not the man who gets all the activity, it is the sexuality of the dreaming girl. After all, this sexuality is a process of maturing and physical transformation which has something almost violent about it. Sexuality suddenly steers her desires by remote control, diverts them, concentrates them on itself: in a word, sexuality rides into the child's life like an alien yet long-awaited force and transforms everything.

The activity of the girl herself is very slight: she can only comply; by allowing herself to be carried off she is only conferring upon sexuality the power it already possesses. But, even so, there is a moment of choice. The girl is able to decide whether she wants to go with the rider – or whether she has to be carried off.

Reading it this way, we see the knight in shining armour dream as a post-pubertal myth, a very general fantasy about the incursion and power of sexuality in the life of an individual. Even the inevitable white horse now turns out to be more significant than was assumed by us (tasteful, reasonable, and averse as we are to yesterday's kitsch). A motor car or an aeroplane, as opposed to a horse, do not fit so well into the imagery found in sexual mythology, although they are more in keeping with the present day. But as an allusion to sex, the various rhythms of the horse are infinitely more appropriate than a smooth car-ride or looping-the-loop in a jet. (This is another case where progress comes up against certain natural limitations.) Yes, I think the knight dream really does have the quality of a post-pubertal myth. It is widespread and enduring because the process of growing up is always experienced in more or less the same way, that is, as a spring awakening, irrespective of historical time or social class (or at least, there are certain similarities in the way it is experienced by individuals). As a stage in our life and an arena for a variety of experiences, growing up is a firm foundation on which collective dreams can blossom, dreams which are both myth and cliché.

So what do we know so far? Do we know anything other than that the foolish dreamers share a collective wisdom which accurately symbolizes sexuality and its power, indeed its violence, when it first appears in a person's life? We know a little more: young girls pay sexuality a remarkable tribute (in their dreams). They imagine that choosing love will bring about a 'turning-point' and a 'new beginning', an 'abrupt leap out of the time continuum', and then 'resurrection in this world'. In short, they promise themselves everything and more, in any case something quite different, something intoxicatingly new that will come out of fulfilling their physical desires. Is that really so foolish? Or would it be better to see things 'realistically' and to condemn this seventh heaven, along with the knight, to the rubbish-heap of history? Alas, enlightenment has been around for long enough. We, the feminists, come along like new goddesses hurling thunderbolts. No, it is no longer a matter of exposing these dreams as illusions, but of discovering the dream within the illusion, the myth within the cliché. And there is a kind of respect for sexuality expressed in this dream which is in stark opposition to the close friendship which the short-sighted and unquestioning mentality of our time believes it can have with the goddess Venus. This kind of dream gives back to sexuality, sexual love, part of the all-powerful influence which our modern world is no longer prepared to grant it now that it has been freed from taboo and 'medicalized'. In that dream where sexuality has the significance of an existential turning point, it is the last time sexuality is given the recognition it deserves. For surely there is no more appropriate view of sexuality than as a force which *carries us off* to an *unknown destination*.

By questioning the knight-in-shining-armour dream, I promised to throw some light on the relationship, the behaviour of *both* sexes towards sexuality. So what about men? As far as I know, boys have a similar kind of dream about knights. Not as often, not as detailed and not as wild. Their imagination draws more nourishment from career plans, that is, dreams to do with career and advancement are projected onto sexuality – homoerotic competition with other men. But in their dreams about love they too, like the girls, are treated to this excursion into the Middle Ages. And they dream the same story, only the other way round. They do not for example see a boy with a pitcher in his hand coming out of the house ready to meet a beautiful lady who comes by on a horse and pauses just long enough to fall in love, and then pulls the boy onto the horse and rides away with him. No, they too see a man in the dream, a knight. They see *themselves* as the knight on horseback, they see a girl, their future beloved, standing at the door. They dream the same dream, but take the opposite role. If we now employ the scheme of interpretation used above once more, we will learn something about the relationship of men to sexuality.

The mounted armour-clad figure from afar who is destined to do the carrying-off – sexuality – is now embodied by the dreamer. Men identify with sexuality, so it is not possible for them to encounter sexuality as a stranger, an unknown abductor. They can sweep the girl away, but they cannot experience the fear and longing for a 'turning-point' in the shape of sexual love. They are guiding the horse, that is, they know where it is going. For a man, a journey into the empire of the senses is not a voyage of discovery: he knows the destination.

It is well known that sexual pleasure has been portrayed as a purely male potentiality in the history of Western civilization, and even more so since the Enlightenment and since it has been set out conceptually in the work of Freud. Sexuality is equated with masculinity. This interpretation is supported by the knight dream, seen from the male point of view. What are the consequences for sexuality of equating it with masculinity? It is clear that as sexuality is practiced now, the male role within it is the dominant one. This has been said many times before, so I'll leave that aside. There is another important aspect which has not come in for so much discussion. Men – who seem to have 'incorporated' it – have stopped paying any tribute to sexuality, they no longer show it any respect nor confer any power upon it. It is men who maintain that awkwardly close companionship with Venus in the belief that she is an old crony of theirs. They think that Venus, sexuality, can be tamed, that they have long since tamed her, like bridling a horse. And they treat with equal disrespect that part of humanity which they must look at and touch in order to trigger and satisfy their sexual desires, while these same women expect something quite different instead of just being pulled onto a horse in passing and taken along for a very short ride.

What arrogance, what airs of superiority! What else can Venus do but return to the waves in horror. I assume that it is for women's sakes that she stays, because their dreams and hopes are far more deferential and wise. Käthchen von Heilbronn certainly understood what love was about.[1]

But fate requires that girls have to look around for men who really exist to fulfil their desires – this is true at least for the overwhelming majority. Their idea of a 'turning point' is bound up not just with sexuality in general, but also with one man in particular. And at this point their strength (their respect for sexuality as seen in the dream) turns into a weakness. There is hardly a man to be found who shares their boldness – to embark on a journey with an unknown destination. Where they would be risking everything men have taken out an insurance. Where women look forward to rising again in this world, men have already eliminated passion. He has mapped out his career where she thought things would start afresh for her. There will be no more leaping beyond the time continuum on this lame charger as long as men – or their disregard for sexuality – are holding the reins.

But are men really holding the reins? Only for a while. We could
be on the wrong track with our interpretation (horse and knight
equals sexuality) if we thought that men could actually manage to
subject all physical desires (the expression and fulfilment of them)
to their own will merely by equating their instincts with sexuality
itself. The charger is lame, it seems – but that may be just
pretence: sometimes it bolts. Since we are not talking about
individual cases here but about the relationship between the sexes
in general, I will allow myself to take an example from literature to
explain what I mean. Whenever a man of letters notices that
sexuality must no longer be subject to control of the male ego
because of factors inherent in it which resist this control, he writes
one of those depressing, tragic stories, usually in the form of a play,
in which eventually everyone dies for love. *Carmen* and *Lulu* are not
odes to the devil in woman, but displays of a campaign of
vengeance by the goddess Venus who cannot be scoffed at with
impunity forever.

These are the facts. Until young men begin to dream of a shining
lady on horseback, until they learn to dream *their* own woman-in-
shining-armour dream, until they can see themselves waiting for a
'turning point' which sexuality would bring about, the goddess
Venus will continue to endure their insults or to seek vengeance,
because she is not satisfied with being revered by only half of
humanity.

Of course, a lot more could be said about these dreams, but let us
leave it at that and try to draw some conclusion. The women's
movement, or women in the movement have stopped having these
dreams since we went our own way and we have laughed out loud
when we remembered them. If you think how many women slid off
the other side of the horse, or were dragged along by the horse's tail
or – most of them – panted along trying to keep up with horse and
rider, then you have to admit that we were right to stop having
these dreams and to laugh about them. But now, remembering that
the rider is identified with sexuality, we should pause and tell
ourselves that the males who offered to sweep us off our feet were
probably the wrong ones. In spite of all its cheap romanticism, the
image of the mounted rider sweeping us along nevertheless has a
certain dignity and we have not escaped punishment for offending

this dignity in the past. If I may put it like this, horse and rider have suffered enough from being usurped by men who wanted to reduce the power of love to their vassal, the shining knight to a projection of their own stupid selves and the white steed to a pedestal for themselves. They have become so out of breath that if they tried to carry us off again, we would only be able to manage a little hop instead of the great leap. Let us give them time to recover. It is one of the unspoken merits of women that they have played no part (or a much, much smaller part) in debasing sexuality by identifying with it in crude camaraderie. The respect that we retained for sexual love may have brought us only the rare moment of sensual pleasure, but it also spared us from the surrogate of sensual pleasure, the casual, almost tedious thrill here and there. Is women's long period of frustration not merely the other side of the coin, i.e. our resistance against stripping love of its enchantment and making it banal? Whatever else the sexual emancipation of women achieves, it should not contribute to the debasement of love.

I do not want to see that happen because I see us women as priestesses of love, or even as martyrs once again, but also because abandoning that 'reverence' (the male form of emancipation) is no use. Anyone who tries to manipulate horse and rider will not be taken anywhere any more, they will not reach that 'unknown destination'. Instead they will remain where they always were, at home with their parents. Perhaps the Oedipus complex is after all simply a reaction to the attempt by the bourgeoisie to domesticate sexuality? The men of the bourgeois age have tried to get hold of the knight's secret, that unknown destination. This did not work -- the horse trotted around in circles. There was nothing new, no turning point, no resurrection in this world. Now we should get the men to climb down off their high horse and admit defeat. We women do not have to correct very much about our own position. We are standing there with our pitcher, ready for that eye-to-eye contact. We are waiting for a shining figure. That shining figure is not you, Count Wetter, it is sensual love itself. It is up to us to choose with whom we wish to ride on the horse's back, be it a man or a woman or even the Holy Spirit for all I care. What is important is that neither of the riders should presume to know where the journey will take them. *Both* of them must be able to say 'Nothing is the same as it was before and the future is uncertain.'

Notes

1   *Das Käthchen von Heilbronn* is a romantic drama, written by the German writer Heinrich von Kleist (1777–1811) in 1808. It is the story of a young girl, Käthchen, who follows with a sort of somnambulistic love and blind devotion the hero knight Graf Wetter vom Strahl. After at first refusing her violently and ruthlessly, he finally falls in love with her, conquered by the constancy of her feelings. [Ed.]

8

The Abortion Law and the Right to Freedom from Bodily Harm

> I have tried to show that men, who alone are responsible for existing laws, are not attempting to protect existent life with Paragraph 218 but that for them it is only a matter of making it impossible for growing women to develop independently in mind and body; that for men it is only a matter of marking off the inner realms of the female body by means of legislation to make them the domain of male enterprise.
>
> Frank Wedekind[1]

'All men are created equal.' When human rights were formulated, they were not intended to extend to women. Democracy is male. Women were not allowed to come of age because they . . . well, why not? The answers I find in feminist literature restate the question – women are not covered by the term 'subject in law' *because* they are women.[2] And why are women women?

We have become accustomed to arguing a sociological case. Facts of nature no longer have a place in the socialized world. And then we are suddenly faced with questions to which the sociological answers seem infuriatingly circular: '. . . because the patriarchy was dominant'. It is true that history has, as it were, absorbed human nature and has specified it in a way which makes it very difficult to make general statements which do anything more than state the obvious. But the obvious is not unimportant just because it is not specific. The fact that women are able to have children is generally true, it is obvious, it can only be modified by history as to how and where it takes place, but the fact itself is unchanged – unless you consider the test-tube baby a realistic prospect which will break the link between women and the ability to have children. This ability to give birth is a fact of nature – yet also, as a concept and object for consideration, it is of great significance, for instance, when trying to explain why women had no say for so long through no fault of their own, and why it is only in the twentieth century that they are beginning to transform human rights into women's rights. Because of its ability to produce another body within itself and to bring this forth, the female body is a completely different physical entity from the male body. It is, as it were, the more physical of the two. All men are created equal, but women are different. The ability to bear children does not allow the female body any arbitrary function. Thus it remains the more defined body. And more than that, in comparison to the male body, it is the weaker of the two in the physical sense. It was a vain *tour de force* when the women's movement tried to explain away women's lesser physical strength by citing sexually specific social conditioning. The relative smallness and delicacy of the female body can only be explained with biology, it is a fact of nature -- an annoying one perhaps, but an inescapable one too.

In short, when human beings rose up at the beginning of modern times to recognize the nature around them and within themselves, to tame it and to exploit it, the men had an inestimable advantage over women: their bodies played a less important part in their lives. And even when their bodies did play a part, their lives were still easier, less disturbed and more predictable. There were no rhythms, no biological tides forcing them to obey their bodies and to abandon other intentions in favour of this obedience. Their bodies remained much the same, apart from the slow processes of natural decay. Their body was a (relatively) reliable basis for bursts of vigour and imagination. In the case of women, the manifold considerations which their bodies demanded from them constituted an obstacle which was biological, yet which had grave historical consequences when the Middle Ages came to an end. The rhythms and relative delicacy of the female body might have been compensated for – there are after all superior features of the female body like, for instance, its better physiological adaptability and its greater endurance. But the great changes taking place in this body, pregnancy, doubling in size, dividing, these catastrophic body-quakes accompanied always by hopes and fears and sometimes by sexual pleasure, kept women confined to bed – marriage-bed, childbed, sick-bed, death-bed, grave.

If women wanted to break out of the existence forced on them by their function in nature, then they had to wait for the men, or for the gains which the men brought back from the front line of the battle against nature. Only now that we are all standing around bewailing our pyrrhic victory over nature do women have their hands on the basic things they need to emancipate themselves from the inertia which their body exerts on their existence – modern medicine and obstetrics, the various methods of contraception. Only one thing is missing, and that is no small matter – the right to abortion.

When the women's movement began twelve years ago, it took a critical look at these 'gains'. It rejected the pill without questioning the need for contraception in general, it attacked hi-tech obstetrics without playing down the risks of giving birth at home (though this was done), they pilloried the big business built up around caring for the female body without discarding modern hygiene. Their concern was essentially that women themselves should control the conditions in which they released their existence from the inertia of their bodies, instead of offering themselves up to industry and medicine.

To say that they actually wanted to release themselves from this inertia may be regarded as controversial by some more extreme branches of feminism, but hardly by mainstream feminism, the effective social movement which moulds people's opinions. Women's emancipation depends on successfully breaking out of the restrictions imposed by nature which women are continually made to endure because they have the ability to produce new life. On their way out of this disadvantaged position, women must accept that their bodies will become more like men's, that their natural rhythms will be suppressed by hygienic, medical and other aids (particularly contraceptive aids) and that these aids will have a profound effect on the female life cycle. Provided this is successful – and we have already made quite a lot of progress particularly in the last two decades – women will no longer be 'confined to bed', but will have the right to make their own decisions concerning their bodies.

Although I understand the argument put forward by minorities in the women's movement (one which ties in with the arguments put forward by politically conservative commentators) which says that if women were to give up their 'difference' they would be giving up a source of potential happiness, it nevertheless seems to me that the majority in the women's movement is right historically in demanding emancipation from that inertia of the body in particular. There is no route to emancipation which does not require a (partial) approximation of the conditions in which the two sexes live in relation to their bodies. Women must leave the horizontal position once and for all. They must make use of the scientific and technical refinements of our civilization to emancipate themselves (still only partially) from biology. They must defend the versatility, flexibility and readiness of their bodies – a readiness to leap into the world 'outside' and to stand tall there – which they possess as children, against the changes brought on by puberty which are intended to re-orientate them into the horizontal position. They must counteract this crippling inertia with a certain corrective restraint.

The movement away from the natural determinism of woman-hood has been a general tendency in the West, with occasional setbacks, for the past hundred years. There is no turning back, however much we may want to, now that the fatal consequences of dominating nature loom on the historical horizon. In a world so just, equal rights require everyone to be willing and able to share equal obligations. That does not necessarily mean that women have to be equal to men in all things. It can also mean, conversely, that men should meet women half-way, that they should take some of that inertia from women (for example by looking after the babies). But essentially the route to be taken is clear – instead of closing in on the bed, women should move away from it in a variety of alternative directions. But the emancipation of women from the inertia of their bodies should also allow them to benefit from this inertia. This will only happen when they have increased their influence on the 'world outside'. Only then will there be grounds for hoping that favourable conditions will be created for experiencing and enjoying to the full those female abilities which stem from this inertia. There are many reasons for emancipating ourselves from biology and one of those (though not the primary one) is that it allows women to return temporarily to the jurisdiction of their bodies when they choose to do so (for example, when they would like to have a child). Thus emancipation from biology could also be seen as a roundabout way of submitting to the laws of biology – but the reward of happiness promised by the conservatives and romantic feminists is only complete because this submission is no longer enforced.

As long as there is no infallible method of contraception while abortion is still subject to legal sanction – in other words, as long as motherhood can still be enforced – women (potentially all women, but in real terms too many) are not of age. They are sacrificed to their biological function. The heaviest weight dragging a woman's body down is the embryo. Only when she has the freedom to rid herself of it will woman herself be free.

The main body of opposition to abortion is the Catholic Church. This institution no longer overtly admits to opposing abortion as a way of conserving its traditional sexual policy: namely excommunicating pleasure and leaving procreation as the sole purpose of sexuality. Instead, the opponents of abortion usually defend their position by taking up the cause of the unborn child. They plunge into a metaphysical debate on the value of life itself. Those in favour of abortion then respond to this with a no less metaphysical discussion about when animate life begins (not before the third month, not before the egg has become implanted in the womb, etc.). Or they launch a couple of diversionary attacks on the lack of concern shown by the conservatives and the clerics for life after birth (the 'cannon-fodder argument'). I should make it clear that we cannot get the better of anti-abortionists who take up the cause of life. Even the germ cells are living things and by destroying the product of their union you destroy life. The *pro-vita* argument is inherently irrefutable. But it is possible and necessary to question this level of argument. We can isolate its metaphysical aspects and show how inappropriate they are for solving the abortion question.

The opponents of abortion – like for instance, the unspeakable sociologist Norbert Martin[3] – set themselves up to defend a life, which they say is 'indivisible'. Yet that life, that embryonic life, is indeed divided, that is to say, it has no reproductive capacity of its own: it is *parasitic*. Almost all the arguments advanced by committed opponents of abortion neglect to mention this self-evident and very significant fact. The unborn child forms a physiological unit with the mother's body; and (in contrast to the mother's body) it is not an autonomous life form in the biological sense. In all parasitic relationships there are crisis situations when the further coexistence of the guest and host bodies is at risk. Either they both start a separate life, or they both perish, or one or the other must be sacrificed. In this sense, every unborn life is a dependent or relative life, something which has always influenced the legal standpoint concerning its protection. The human community, or our society, has created its own regulations – regulations for deciding for and against, and for mediating and striking a balance between the different 'parties' in the parasitic community. And these regulations determine what should be done in individual cases. What we must do is change these regulations and, if possible, take away their status as part of the law altogether. It is not a question of asserting or denying 'life', of approving or defending an act of killing. The individual woman's refusal to allow her body to be used as a host body must now be the foremost of these crises between 'guest and host bodies', and overcoming this crisis presents a completely different set of problems (logically and historically speaking) from the comparatively abstract question of whether it is legitimate to kill an independent life. The shameless propaganda put about, particularly by the Church and right-wing conservatives, equating abortion with genocide, should itself be brought to justice and added to the list of punishable offences.

Conflicts between the bodies of embryo and mother are, speaking subjectively, always conflicts experienced by the mother, and the way these conflicts are resolved in our society could quite easily be 'de-legalized', that is, removed from the purview of the penal code altogether. The state would then abstain from judgement and would leave it entirely up to the persons concerned whether they wanted to continue with their pregnancy or not. This is precisely what the women's movement was demanding when its banners called for the abortion law to be struck off the statute books entirely. By de-legalizing abortion in this way, i.e. by returning control of all the conditions of reproduction to private citizens, female and male, the basic legal rights – above all the *right to freedom from bodily harm* – would at last extend to *all* people.

For when human rights were formulated, the term 'body' referred to the male body. The right to freedom from bodily harm did not extend to women. With the anti-abortion laws and social pressure to have children, women were constantly expected to tolerate being controlled by others through the medium of their bodies. They had no choice but to submit to their fate, their natural function. After all, what was the Enlightenment, the individualization of civilized human beings in modern times, if not a kind of emancipation from the fate which nature determined or which was determined by one's circumstances at birth, a route already mapped out through the 'valley of the shadow of death'. When considering the 'backwardness' of women in the face of the modern world's demands (mobility, flexibility, rationality, etc., however critically we view these demands), there is really only this one trivial fact which we keep coming back to – inertia of the body. Women's bodies continued to be opened, distended and transformed into a kind of hostel and milk factory entirely against the will of the individuals concerned,[4] even after the right to freedom from bodily harm was set down in the first modern constitutions and the gentry could be taken to court for beating their tenant farmers.

'Oh come on', the argumentative anti-abortionist says at this point, 'there is after all a difference between hitting someone with a riding-crop and a woman having a baby.' A difference in what respect? We're talking about human rights here, or more precisely, about the constitution of West Germany and there in *Article 2.2* it says that every human being has a right to freedom from bodily harm. Is it not an infringement of this right if a woman is expected to submit to a pregnancy and give birth to a child she never wanted? There is also pleasure to be gained from reproducing – but this is not automatically the case. Like all (possible) pleasure, it turns into the extreme opposite of pleasure – panic, revulsion, despair – if the thing which can cause it (in this case, pregnancy) interrupts at the wrong moment or in the wrong social context. 'And what about the unborn child's right to freedom from bodily harm?' No, let's not have any of this metaphysical discussion (see above). The opponent of abortion smiles at this point. He does not even have to have the last word, so convinced is he that heartfelt common sense is on his side. 'You can say what

you like, but it is scorning God's creation to equate pregnancy with
bodily harm.'

In my opinion, you are scorning the Enlightenment *and* religious
faith if you drag in creation, the Lord God and all the trappings of a
long-defunct reverence for 'some higher power' to justify the law
which forces women to submit to their biological destiny. The
problem facing us today is one of the basic rights – the necessity for
women at last to have an equal share in the blessings, however
mixed, conferred by the Magna Charta and all the other gains won
by the genius of that age.

When human rights were born, the rights of personal freedom,
the idea of *equality* was also developed. Much of the social and
political progress which we would still like to regard as such today
relates to this idea as the centre around which it is structured.
There could not be an antidiscrimination movement which was not
based on the idea of equality. If the abortion law were to disappear,
we would be rid of one of the oldest and most resistant guarantees
of inequality in relation to the opportunities open to individuals to
develop as sexual beings. As equals, women would be freer in two
ways: firstly, they could take an active part in professional and
personal life independently of their reproductive capabilities, as has
long been the norm for men. And secondly, they could have
recourse to their reproductive capability when *they* chose to. They
would at last be able to develop this ability and take pleasure in it.
In other words, only the freedom to have an abortion would make
women free to have children when they wanted.

The fact remains that the opponents of abortion consider it
unreasonable to equate unwanted pregnancy with bodily harm.
They still see pregnancy as the work of God which cannot be
altered by basic rights. 'After all, you cannot put a man who
impregnates a woman on a par with violent criminals or rapists.'
Nor do I intend to do so, but I can see that by referring to *Article
2.2*, I might give that impression. But this is only true as long as
abortion remains a punishable offence. Things could be rectified by
making abortion free to all and this would also lessen the problem
of unwanted pregnancies. Society would then grant women a
kind of compensation for their particular physical vulnerability,
albeit by way of a new kind of bodily harm, abortion itself, but one

which 'encroaches' nowhere near as much as enforced motherhood.

As long as abortion is not free to all, we cannot say that every man who sleeps with a woman is potentially guilty of bodily harm, but we can say that society makes itself guilty of tolerating a serious case of discrimination – that is, (partly) excluding women from the protection given by a basic right.

Just because pregnancy is a 'natural process' does not mean that it should not be considered as an encroachment on physical integrity when it is unwanted. Ageing, death and complications at birth are also 'natural', yet in these cases we put nature right with a clear conscience as far as is possible. And the fact that women themselves play a part in conception, virtually aiding and abetting what could be a 'grave' infringement of their own physical integrity, makes it even more necessary to eradicate the abortion law. The conflict between the search for pleasure, metaphysical morality and fear of public punishment has prevented women from developing their ability to love for long enough.

A look at the anti-abortion arguments shows how deeply entrenched this discrimination still is. In the first place, the reference to God's creation makes it quite clear where in history women came to a standstill – at a time where there were still gods (as the magical incarnations of an unfathomed, unpenetrated dependence on nature). As long as god continues to be cited in justification for the abortion law, women will continue, even in the twentieth century, to live out certain phases of their existence somewhere between the plague and the inquisition. Secondly, the fact that during the constitutional debate on the reform of the abortion law in West Germany there could still be serious talk of unacceptable 'egoism' on the part of those women who wanted to shun motherhood is an indication of the same time-lag. The Magna Charta Libertatum marked the beginning of an age when the selfishness of individuals was accepted as something not only *there* but as something legitimate as well and this selfishness has influenced or even underpinned all the relevant codes and discourses of the modern bourgeois consciousness, from economics to modern civil law. This is not an analogy, but *proof* of the fact that women are constantly being pushed back into the Middle Ages, as it were, whenever they stand up for equality. Because it was precisely that egoism alluded to in the abortion debate which was at stake when the individual was involved in the political and ideological struggle to obtain personal rights: the interest in one's personal well-being ('pursuit of happiness' as it was called during the American Revolution).

I should add that in earlier times, tying women down to their biological function had a certain 'point' to it for the survival of the species. The chances of the offspring surviving birth and the first few years were small and for that reason there was an 'objective' desire to have a lot of children. In the meantime, the prognostics have reversed: there is now a real threat of over-population. This being the case, even 'objectively' speaking, it is completely out of step with the times to continue to protect the human species in the same way. As far as the law is concerned, this protection would seem to find its justification in the collective memory of those hard times long ago.

By concentrating the debate on the child (whether it is to be kept or aborted) attention has been diverted from the fact that the unwanted pregnancy itself is a state of being controlled by others through the medium of the body, indeed a state of captivity which is incompatible with the guarantees offered by civil liberties. The unwanted child is 'only' a threat, albeit a very serious one; but pregnancy is an immediate phenomenon and when unwanted it always assumes the dimensions of a personal catastrophe. The official abortion debate overlooked and continues to overlook this fact; it is only interested in whether motherhood can be enforced or not. It ought also to be interested in whether it is permissible to enforce *pregnancy* upon women. I do not think the legitimacy of the demands for free abortion should be allowed to rest solely, or even primarily, on social justifications. Certainly the long-term social, economic and other changes which motherhood brings into any woman's life are profound enough to be unacceptable if they occur against the will of the individual involved (at least an individual protected by civil liberties), but these changes are not the only points which must be raised in opposition to the abortion law, nor are they even the most important if we are considering the right to freedom from bodily harm. Opponents of abortion are always pointing out that mothers soon grow to love their children even if they did not really want them at first. Well, all credit for this pleasing state of affairs goes to the children, not to the abortion law. Any adjustment made .after the event to deal with motherhood should not divert attention from decisions which individuals may make before the event in opposition to motherhood. Norbert Martin is a good example of someone who continues to do this:

> During the period of pregnancy, particularly the first months, the woman is particularly unstable, spiritually and emotionally. She may want an abortion, but if she bows to 'gentle pressure' from a responsible doctor, then experience often shows that later she is glad she did so, because afterwards she receives her child with the full power of her womanly emotion.[5]

Such bogus arguments are an attempt to justify necessity with the virtue born of necessity; and to ensure that such arguments are not so readily accepted in future, I think it is important to move one step back and ask if it is admissible to enforce pregnancy (let alone birth) – in other words, whether a woman ought to be prevented from using existing methods to put things right. I do not think women should ever be expected to accept a pregnancy which takes place in a body forced to comply with the situation, a pregnancy which is unacceptable to a consciousness motivated solely by a desire to re-establish its former physical boundaries. I do not think women should ever be expected to accept this pollution of their bodies by an inexorable fertility programme whose machinations put blood, tissue and nerves into uproar and the poor self into shame and agony, a physical revolt which is totally uncalled for. Women who do not want to should not be put into this physical condition for any longer than is necessary for diagnosis and treatment. Can we take guarantees of personal freedom seriously as long as psychophysical beatings such as unwanted pregnancy are tolerated? Women request abortion when they do not want a child, that is certainly true. But they also request it because they do *not want to be pregnant* (let alone become a mother). Admittedly, this distinction is a purely theoretical one. But it is more than just pedantic. Such a distinction will help me to extract what, for me, is most important: a woman's ability to control her own body. I do not mean just in the long term (whether or not to have children, how many, etc.) but also in the short term, so that her body is her own and does what she wants, here and now.

Abortion ought at last to be possible with no legal strings attached. Saying that abortion itself violates the female body is not an argument in favour of the abortion law, but another indication of how important it is to remove the female body, vulnerable as it is because of its reproductive role, from the influence of the penal code and finally to make it subject to nothing other than the will of individual women. In other words, it shows how necessary it is to extend civil liberties to women too. Up till now the legislators have been more interested in the reproductive function itself: it was this they wanted to protect, against the will of individuals if necessary. We must turn their attention to the female body and show them that it is subject to independent will in the same way that a man's is. What we must do is in a way *restore the virginity* of the female body in the eyes of the law and the constitution. The ability of individual women to reproduce, or activating that ability, must be as personal a matter as one's own sexual preferences. The legislator should be responsible only for ensuring that the preconditions and consequences of sexuality, as far as they affect the body, are controlled by individual women and by what those women want. As long as 'nature' or God is allowed to press the female body into service without asking permission, women will continue to be innocent victims with no say of their own, rather than modern, independent individuals.

'Male' democracy is imperfect not only because it excludes half of humanity from enjoyment of certain personal liberties, but also (inasmuch as it is *willing* to include women, at least today) because it has committed a basic error of logic. A guarantee of right is only truly general or even absolute, when it is oriented towards those members of the group it protects who are in the most unfavourable position to avail themselves of it. A fortress defended by a moat and ramparts offers protection to its inhabitants even if there is no law of trespass, but the same is not true for a tenement block. The fortress of the male body is not so easy to violate: a simple guarantee clause would be enough to protect it. The unshielded and fragile female body, which is much more directly exposed to menace and encroachment by man and nature, requires a more complex legal apparatus to protect it. When the Magna Charta was formulated, it was inconceivable for the first bourgeois thinker to profane the blessing of children by seeing it as something undesirable: here nature and religion imposed tight restrictions on political speculation. Since then we have become much the wiser. Social morality and individual preferences have changed dramatically. Women see their generative role as one among many and more and more women are only prepared to play that role if they are no longer forced to do so.

The time is ripe for reformulating the basic right to freedom from bodily harm. And this time it is the female body which must serve as the model. How are we going to set about making sure that modern constitutions protect this body? In other words, how can we guarantee that the will of women themselves retains sole authority over their bodies? Once this will is free to act, it will, I hope, send God packing first. But I hope that it will also be indulgent towards lovers and children, as it wishes.

As it wishes – not as responsibility requires? The fathers of the American constitution knew what they were about when they coined that phrase, 'the pursuit of happiness'. The day the last judge, priest or politician is ashamed to use the word 'responsibility'[6] with respect to women and their bodies will be the first day that women, all women, are allowed to pursue 'happiness' in the eyes of the law. That day is certainly still a long way off. And it will not dawn as long as the abortion law continues to exist.

Notes

1   Frank Wedekind (1864–1918) is one of the most radical German dramatists of the turn of the century. Amongst other plays he wrote *Frühlings Erwachen* (Zürich, J. Gross, 1891) and the *Lulu* tragedies (Munich, A. Langen, 1895), in which he severely attacked the sexual repression and hypocrisy of the Wilhelmean era.

In the legal code of West Germany, paragraph 218 regulates the question of abortion. Until the seventies abortion had always been a criminal offence except where there were strong medical grounds, in which case abortion might be provided free of charge. After the coalition between the Social Democrats and Liberals came into power in 1969 the long-standing feminist and progressive struggle to establish social grounds as a rationale for free abortion was successful. Though that represented a crucial step forward in the fight for free abortion, there has been ever since a determined counter-attack. This counter-attack is informed by the ethics of the Catholic Church. It is backed increasingly in political debates by today's Conservative/ Liberal government. This has immediate practical results, as it feeds the possible refusal to terminate a pregnancy by certain hospitals and individual doctors, especially in the traditionally Catholic *Länder* like Bavaria or Baden-Württemberg. At the moment the Conservatives are attempting to change legislation in order to withdraw the financial support of the National Health insurance scheme from abortions provided on social grounds. This would of course hit women from the lower social strata severely. [Ed.]

2   Hannelore Schröder (ed.), *Die Frau ist frei geboren. Text zur Frauen-emanzipation*, Munich, Oscar-Beck, 1979, vol. 1, p. 14.

3   In Dietrich Hoffmann (ed.), *Schwangerschaftsunterbrechung. Aktuelle Übelegungen zur Reform des § 218*, Frankfurt, Suhrkamp, 1974, p. 218.

4   No one is denying that women have voluntarily given in to inertia, perhaps even often. We are not dealing with Egmont's Klärchen here, but with Hebbel's Klara. It is no loss to the former if the latter wins.

5   From Hoffman (ed.), p. 222.

6   If it is responsibility they are worried about, what about the responsibility towards children? After all, they do indeed have a right to be wanted.

9

Differences and Similarities Between the Sexes

One of the logical tasks facing the feminist movement in its role as a consciousness-raising school was and still is to create a concept of 'femininity': women should have their own particular energy, intelligence, mind and sexuality. But since feminism was and is also a movement against discrimination, it has always been involved in a fight against false specifications, saying that as far as energy, intelligence, feeling and sexuality are concerned, we claim equal rights because we possess essentially equal potentiality. Well, what now? Is the female sex 'different' or 'the same'? It is the same, and yet different from the male sex – but not in the way the patriarchy would have it. Perhaps the male sex is also different from what it thinks it is and hopefully it will not be more equal than the female sex for much longer. In any case, since the female sex has always been the negative image of male self-definition, the male sex will become different as the female sex changes – and the female sex is changing radically in order to be itself at last.

As a political, social and cultural movement, feminism has a hard time trying to reconcile this simultaneous identity and polarity. Feminists are forever having to do a bit of both – pressing for equality and yet emphasizing the difference, insisting on identity and yet asserting our position in this polarity. It started when we demanded equal rights to vote, and continued when we became trainees and now that some of us have attained professional status it is most important: if we demand equal rights, we are assuming that our ability to make political decisions, to gain qualifications and to practise a profession, etc. are equal to those of men. There is a nice line from a children's song which says 'Girls are just as naughty as boys, just as daring, just as strong, etc.'

On the other hand, feminist criticism is compelled to preserve the differences, or even to produce them in the first place. We do not want to perpetuate the aggressive and competitive world of men, nor should we. Equal rights – female Utopias – both arms of this dialectic pincer must hold fast. If one arm of the pincer is ineffective, the result will be either affirmation or escapism.

The women's movement started, I think, with the first critical victory, which was seizing the male domains of professional and public life and in particular, depending on the class from which the members of the movement came, gaining qualifications in politics, science, art, etc. In other words, the main demand at the beginning was for equality. This old revolutionary slogan of the middle classes which has its good and bad sides, has been with the women's movement since it began (again) about one hundred years ago. The slogan demands that women be given their long-overdue civil liberties in practice. We have since realized that human rights were men's rights, they did not extend to the world of women. We have now been working for a hundred years to make human rights applicable to all and to gain the status of 'human being' for ourselves as women. And that's where the problem starts – do we really want to be 'human beings'? Do we need this 'status' which has been developed by the patriarchy in the course of its history and is therefore inferior? Is it worth striving for?

At any rate, the male human being, or humanity – male-dominated and therefore defined as male – has developed through history at the expense of its female part, sacrificing the development of this part. It was therefore able to bring about human development and civilization while or because it excluded and despised one part of itself in what seemed an almost natural way. On this point there is a very simple and therefore very trenchant statement by Simone de Beauvoir in which she demonstrates by means of an analogy just how scandalous it is that women have been deprived of their rights for thousands of years:

> Our enthusiasm for the democracy of ancient times is quickly tempered when we realise that its socioeconomic basis was slavery. What are we to think of all the social and economic progress of modern times if we consider that this progress has never really

happened for women and that no one has accounted for this fact –
just as in antiquity, the free men did not think about the price of
their freedom?

Fair enough, so we hesitate before pursuing our demand for
equality because we have to ask ourselves whether we really want
this equality.

But we still demand it.

The key to this problem is that by demanding, fighting for and finally gaining equality, we change the conditions under which 'human
beings' now men *and women* with equal rights, enjoy their rights.

What I'd like to stress is that that moment of hesitation –
figuratively speaking – serves an important purpose: in this
moment of hesitation, this period of consideration, there occurs a
process by which a kind of female self-awareness is created. A kind
of self-awareness which does not become absorbed in demands for
equality, but which sets us apart and makes us different. In other
words, it takes a critical view of patriarchal history. At first sight it
would appear that this process is a negative activity – it happens as
a result of rejection. We all know that this gesture of rejection was
not enough for the women's movement and that we have been
working for some time on a way of making our self-awareness into
something positive, of filling a seemingly empty space in the history
of womankind. It is a history of deprivation and exclusion, but it
would not be a history at all if there had not also been some kind of
positive development within it, if there was nothing to report about
what women really have *done* in the last 2000 years. This difficult
task, part archaeology, part excavation to expose an empty space in
history which could be called 'womanhood', preoccupies a number
of minds in the women's movement. Sometimes the desire for a
positive history is the mother of great flights of fancy into the
matriarchal times of pre- and early history; as time goes on it will
become clear which research findings we can trust and which we
cannot (by the way, it is normally the case that desires are what
give rise to research projects, desires which in some way prefigure
the results).

The moment of hesitation prevents us from immediately carrying
out our intention to demand equality and only allows us to pursue

our aim when various projects have been set up to answer the question of how desirable equality is. This moment of hesitation is to a certain extent responsible for the 'change in conditions' which I mentioned above. It is responsible for the fact that the demands for equality are not made uncritically; that women also remain 'different' while being 'equal'.

Again and again it has been observed and has been the object of regret that the women's movement 'is splitting into two sections'. There is a more politically oriented section which has inherited the old emancipation programme and which is out for equal opportunities favouring practical solutions, and there is a section which is at pains to seek a historical identity and for which equality is not enough. This 'second' section is concerned with the particular, the 'female' and is not so concerned with short-term successes. The polemics continue according to the point of view: one section says these ambitious emancipators are nothing more than career women who expect other women to waste their better talents in a fruitless male-determined competition while the other section says that women who are concerned with femininity as a specific thing are falling prey to reactionary obscurantism which makes it easy for sexists to write off the feminist cause entirely. That is more or less how the dispute continues today – what are we to say to that?

For me it goes against the grain to condemn the dispute too severely. It seems reasonable to treat the whole controversy as something unnecessary: the truth is we need both approaches, the pragmatic one and the Utopian one, the political one and the aesthetic one, the one which insists on equality and the one which insists on difference. After all, the structure or techniques of feminist criticism could be seen as a 'dialectic pincer'. But apparently this pincer is made up not only of two arms, the two approaches themselves – there is also a certain polemical tension between the two. In a way, there is no point in trying to reconcile the two halves. The internal feud clarifies and outlines the positions and the level of criticism, therefore also the level of the work and the characteristics of each approach. Integration of the two approaches could at best come about through what we call practical activity.

This necessity to consider equality and difference of the sexes at the same time has consequences for the programme followed by feminism as well as for the methodology of feminist criticism. Take the words 'equal rights'. They imply that the group demanding equal rights is willing to take on equal obligations and to carry out the same tasks as those who are privileged to have the rights already. How does that look in practice? Can women really achieve the same as men in all or nearly all areas of so-called human practice? I think the fact that we are gradually less and less concerned with this hoary old chestnut is an indication of the fact that it has already been decided: yes, women really can do the same as men. Girls really can be as naughty as boys. The worrying thing is, they *are not* as naughty as boys. If we ask why this should be so, we of course conclude that social conditions are still a long way from real equality, starting with the education young girls receive and continuing with the fact that women who have been only housewives and mothers are cheated out of old age pensions.

At the same time girls seem to have more opportunity to develop a naughty streak or women more opportunity to follow careers than one would suppose if one considered the modest extent to which women are conspicuous to the public. If we look at the majority we will find, I think, that women's restraint is a result of that potentiality which is an important basic reason for the divergence of the sexes into two different worlds: women's ability to have children. We come back to biology. Or to the fact that the emancipation of 'humanity' (if we might be so bold as to take humanity as a whole) from nature is illusory.

Not only are women as capable as men, they are more capable. This 'more' means that they are less capable. Before I myself had a child, I did not realize how difficult it is to combine a professional career with having a child. It is possible, but, even now, it is incredibly difficult. The fact that there are many childless women who prefer to hide in the home instead of doing something sensible or even becoming feminists, does not, I think, contradict my argument: the enormous shortage of courage which we can see in women, to go out and to compete with men in public and professional life, is deeply rooted in the social and psychological demands which motherhood involves and which seems to suck out the female life-force; it tends to consume the whole woman.

We have seen then that the demand for equal rights founders on a real biological inequality. The consequence of this state of affairs, as seen by Shulamith Firestone, must be enthusiastic support for test-tube babies. This conclusion is absolutely logical but no more than that. I would prefer a conclusion which had some historical support. If we take a look at how unsuccessful biology has been at forcing the human species to remain within its prescribed boundaries, I am optimistic. Although biologically we are not equipped for it, we launch ourselves into the air, dive into the deep sea, etc. I don't see why it shouldn't be possible for humans to find ways of relieving women of their permanent and exclusive responsiblity for children without restricting their biological potential, without taking away from them that bit extra they possess: the ability to give birth. In other words, we must do away with the social consequences of the inequality in generative functions. It only needs someone to put a bit of imagination and initiative into these problems. Men will not do it because they are quite happy with fatherhood being a subsidiary role in their lives. Here, then, women have a wonderful opportunity to prove their socially innovative capabilities. I know that feminists have long been working on initiatives to get the abortion law abolished and on ways of easing the burden for mothers, but there is still not enough being done. If equal rights really do presuppose an ability to bear equal obligations, then the consequences of biological inequality must be nipped in the bud and redistributed equally between the sexes – otherwise equality remains but a nice idea.

There is only a real inequality between the sexes in terms of anatomy, sexuality, the reproductive function and the psychological reflexes of it – in every other aspect equality is possible. And even within sexuality, the polarity may be even more than just complementary: I have the suspicion that Eros loves metamorphoses and when he takes charge it is never laid down quite definitively to which sex an individual belongs. I'll come back to this.

The basic biological difference between the sexes only really matters in those cases where it serves a particular purpose, for instance in the sex act. And yet in practice, it seems to matter a lot more. By making itself out to be so important, it influences every aspect of society, colouring and interfering with it even when those involved believe they are disregarding it. An individual's gender is the very first piece of information that the individual gives us when we meet her/him, and it is sometimes also the last – if that individual is a woman. If the individual is a man, the piece of information gives way to a variety of further information. In the case of women, their gender is the main issue, with men it is just one of many features. This lack of symmetry is a product of the male perspective on the world which is unable to draw a straight axis. When men think of woman, they think of one thing only, i.e. they are interested in her as a sexual being; in all other matters they assume, mainly, that they will be dealing with other men.

As the viewpoint of the dominant members of society is the dominant viewpoint, and therefore women too look at things in this distorted way, the lack of symmetry scarcely remains limited to particular occasions. It comes about that the information we women carry before us as sexual beings speaks louder than it does for men, that it drowns out, as it were, anything else we might have to say. Women normally have no opportunity to conceal or forget their femaleness so that they can simply take a share in life. Men are unfamiliar with this problem. In the male world, the information they give to the rest of the world by their gender is, as it were, harmless. Provided they are not courting somebody or trying to get into a women-only bar, they have no reason to fear that that first piece of information will be taken as the only interesting thing about them and reduce anything else they may have to offer to secondary importance. Women, who are supposed to be only women first, then nothing at all for a while and then only women again, must at some point wish that they were not recognizable as women. That is not supposed to mean that they want to be men, but simply that just for once gender should not matter – so that the other things they have to offer can come to the fore.

This kind of imperialism which gender practises, chaining women to their female biology, tends to eradicate the things which distinguish individuals, in other words, that one small difference overshadows the finer differences. The fact that the ever-present polarity of the sexes drones away constantly like a basso continuo drowning out the music of social interaction makes us as female individuals more impoverished than we need be. Our personal talents and abilities only count in the light of our gender, and because of that they count for too little. Since these abilities and talents only stand a chance of being developed if they are noticed, we must assume that much of the potential of individual women never reaches maturity because women are over-identified with their gender. Now, in this field the women's movement has really achieved a great deal. It has created forums where women can learn how to look at each other in a 'different' more discriminating way and reject the prevailing, jaundiced view. I'm talking about places and events where men were not allowed. At these events women were able to perceive each other as teachers, nurses or scientists, as sensitive, considerate or impetuous individuals, as small, fat or tall women, etc. and *not* in the first instance just as a *woman*, as a *non-man*. At a women's congress or at other such events bringing together women exclusively, we can run round without being conspicuous or, for once, we can be conspicuous for some other reason instead of because of our gender primarily. Do men actually know how much it hurts to be conspicuous because of gender, that is, because of a feature which each individual shares with *half of the human race*? (Of course it doesn't always hurt, it can also be a real pleasure, but this side of the dialectic does not belong in this context.)

As I said, over-identifying with gender makes it difficult to perceive and to perceive oneself, thereby making it difficult also to develop personal traits or abilities. But of course, in reality there is no individuality removed from gender. Abstracting away from gender is a purely theoretical process, one which is necessary in order to take a critical look at that process of abstraction from personality (as far as personality is not the same as gender) which for men is in no way limited to the theoretical plane. Excluding men from women's centres, etc. was a first step. We had to create situations where it was no longer possible to reduce things to gender by pushing away the ones doing the reducing. There the dialectics of feminist criticism are very clearly demonstrated: the much-criticized retreat of women to women, a movement which made gender a criterion for belonging, thereby at first overvaluing it, had the precise purpose of bringing an end to the predominance of gender among personal characteristics.

Well, what about difference and equality in sex itself? Is the asymmetry lost at least here? By no means! The only direct line of communication existing between the sexes, sex itself, is quite a frail thing – it means something very different to each of the two worlds. The two sexes in one sense repeat the folly of Babel – they do not understand each other because they do not speak the same language. They do not even understand each other in the situation where one sex is made for the other. Even when they ought to speak the same language, that of sex or sexual love, they talk at cross-purposes because they do not have enough experience in common outside this area. After all, love has a kind of totalitarian impulse: lovers are required to talk about more than just love itself. Nowadays, when the experiences which the two sexes have in all possible affairs is growing more and more equal, it is clear how great is the power of the past – the misunderstandings during embraces are not reduced, or perhaps only now does their full extent become clear. The only language the two sexes have in common does not work because each one intends something different with the same words, because each one interprets intonation, pauses, allusions and *double entendres* in a different way. What makes the situation so confoundedly difficult is that apart from this one common language, which is not common in fact, the dominant sex commands a great number of other modes of discourse from which the inferior sex is excluded. For men who are able to put their ambition, ability, libido, quite simply their whole lust for life and expression to the test in the various fields, provided they are not sex maniacs, the field of sex is of secondary importance. Therefore they have a weaker attachment, a lesser respect for this mode of discourse and for that reason they can tolerate vulgarity, indiscretion, even imbalance and obscenity. After all they do not have to value too highly the partners they communicate with in their capacity as sexual beings: since women speak fewer languages, and since the language of sex which they can only really use with men seems to be their most refined language, men must feel that their partners in the area of sexuality and reproduction were created expressly for this area and to serve them personally. And they react to them in a correspondingly patronizing or openly brutal way. 'The emotion befitting the practice of domination is contempt not reverence', wrote Adorno in answer to the hypocritical bourgeois commandment that men should honour women.

It is a fact that the language of sex has been handed down to us women as our main language. In most other discourses we were allowed to participate only on the sidelines, to stand by and look on, as it were, but we were seldom allowed to get a real command, let alone to master them. No wonder that many of us overload with expectations the one discourse we may, and indeed are, expected to command as sexual beings, paying it the appropriate respect, but overestimating it because it is (almost) our only one. Thus because of the diversity of the demands which each sex places on sexuality, love, having children and bringing them up (sexual existence in its broadest sense) there is no real communication between them. That is the ironic conclusion: in the only language of which the two sexes really do have equal knowledge they cannot communicate *because* it is the only language they have in common.

If women were as fluent in as many languages as men, in other words, if they had really wholly recovered from being reduced to sexual beings, i.e. if they were emancipated, then the two sexes could once again communicate in the language of sexuality too – because this language would be just one of many in both their lives and could therefore be spoken by both sexes with the same relative commitment. It would no longer be the case that everything – or at least, too much – was at stake for one sex and only a little for the other, distorting the discourse and making the voices oscillate at different frequencies, thereby leading to that Babel situation in which each plunges the other into the unhappy circumstance of non-communication.

I have exaggerated somewhat – the reality we experience has long since ceased to be so severe in the mutually exclusive organization of the male and female world; nowadays women go into space and men clean the kitchen. But in opposition to these changes which, happily, are working their way from the margin to the centre of society, there is still the old basic tendency which has a decisive effect.

There is a conservative argument, or rather a conservative interruption, in opposition to the effects which the demand for equality has had on love and sex: if women really achieved full equality, love's mystery would perish: after all, the effects of the women's movement and the youth rebellion are already clear to see – the banishment of the mystical and the introduction of a competitive element into sexuality and love. Yes, as far as what is desirable is concerned, I am in agreement with every conservative: that sexuality and love, the field on which the sexes play out their differences, should remain spared from full rationalization for its very survival. It is just that I see the reasons for this negative development elsewhere. It is not the demand for equality or the first step towards realizing it which makes the language of love and pleasure into jargon, but it is a lack of equality between the sexes which causes us to resort to jargon as a compromise, and to competition as a surrogate for equality.

Let us leave men aside for a moment. As far as women are concerned, the following is true: only when they are no longer obliged to resort to their sexual existence (in the broadest sense) as their 'chief task' will they be able to discover the possibilities and attractions of their existence and find a language for it which is no longer distorted by fear. In order to find love and sex mysterious, one cannot be in an involuntary relationship of serfdom. Sentimentalizing love and demonizing sex are male achievements, yet men always had the possibility of creeping up on the charmed circles from an outer and inner distance. After all, what risk is there if they allow themselves to get a little involved? Women had no choice (or very much more limited options) for they were caught up in that circus of love from the very start. Therefore it is difficult for them to give their sexual existence an air of mystery, as it is their bread and butter. We can only expect them to do this 'voluntarily' i.e. resist competition and jargon, if they too are at least able to *choose* whether sex should play a part in their lives at all and if so, then when, how, with whom, etc.

In other words, as far as women's fate is concerned, only by making it *less important* will the relationship between the sexes take on the characteristics of a major or important matter serving the cause of the 'basic difference'.

Serving the cause of the 'basic difference' – hardly have I written it when I notice how badly this formulation needs to be explained further. The basic difference, or the immutable inequality of the sexes in anatomy, also has the element of illusion and ideology about it. Particularly in the sex act, which is also called 'union', there are many aspects which eradicate the difference or melt it down, for example, at the moment of finding pleasure when in an analogous or perhaps even identical way, both sexes are at the mercy of some third party – a state of ecstasy where the rational can no longer keep up; or in the many variations on the sex act of which the basic principle seems to be an exchange of roles. In short, as I said previously, Eros loves metamorphoses and when he is around, it is never quite fixed which gender an individual belongs to at a particular moment. When I said that, I was getting at the fact that even the natural, biological polarity of the sexes is in a way something relative, something which invites the polarity to be more fluid. Even in situations which are so completely based on inequality such as the sex act, there is a tendency at work to remove this inequality. Perhaps I can put it this way: even that difference which is provided by nature as polarity is not a determining factor, because the sexes can – within certain limitations – exchange their roles. (This fact is important especially for the field of reproduction, as witnessed in the irksome practice of tying women down to looking after children which is justified by ideology, etc.)

When social life in its basic units of love and family life is no longer bound up in stereotypes or an ideology which regards the sexes as polarized in terms of their attributes, then quite different polarities, differences and variations can play a greater part: those of individuals as personalities independent of their gender. A large part of our erotic potentiality lies dormant in these individual features which must be developed beyond the level of belonging to a particular gender. Awakened, they could perhaps help to keep safe the mystery of sexual love, that mystery which so many are worried is being lost today.

In any case, the social inequality between the sexes, the one which affects the development of individuality, is the greatest difference between them. All the biological differences pale in comparison. That's why I think the strongest emphasis in feminist criticism remains on that side of the dialectical pincer which demands equality.

10

The Phantom of 'Female Sexuality'

A few years after it started, the women's movement proudly put forward a very special blueprint – the blueprint of *female sexuality*. It counts as one of the movement's intimate personal documents, it is its passport to autonomy. Compiled from the results of surveys, the critique of psychoanalysis, confessions and dreams, this blueprint outlines the as-yet-unknown female instinct which has still to be liberated. By referring to it, women can foil any attempt by men to talk feminism into a compromise. Women have different feelings. Their enormous potentiality – ignored by male-dominated psycho-analysis, stifled in practice by marriage, diverted by motherhood and degraded in literature as much by excessive sentimentality as by fear-induced demonization of womankind in general – is just at the beginning of its development. Woman is capable of oceanic tides of pleasure, endless orgasms, gentle and tempestuous waves of affection, boundless ecstasy, while all the male sex has to show is its simplistic mechanism of arousal, explosion and relaxation.

Men, apparently redundant from their positions as bedfellows, became both depressed and impressed: they made hardly any reference to the subject without acknowledging the feminist victory. To be on the safe side, they tried to adapt. The result was the 'softy' with '. . . his hands softened by all that caressing' as it was once expressed in the magazine *Titanic*.

The softy has since gone out of fashion. But the feminist blueprint is still on the table. It haunts the realms of love like an ever-present joker with the result that whatever men do they are wrong. Affected virility is ridiculous, aggression taboo, empathy impossible. If woman the lover were ever a sphinx, enigmatic, timeless, insatiable and desirable, she is even more so today. Feminism makes her more demanding and at the same time she is not missing much anyway: men are just not up to it. I allow them to experiment a little, we talk affectionately. Then we go our separate ways: men back into the prison of their imagination which, despite their efforts, remains full of whores, and I one step further on the road to developing my oceanic potentiality. Don't try to follow me, man, you'll only sink. *Au revoir*, or better, *adieu*!

Adieu? Was God really guilty of a flaw in design when he created Adam and Eve, failing to make the two sexually compatible? I find that hard to believe. But let us leave God out of this. It is right that women had good reason to terminate their sexual submissiveness to men. For far too long the female body has been abused as a training ground for patriarchal projections and policies and at some time women had to call a halt to this. But does that justify a blueprint for gender-specific sexuality where the other sex merely rates as an interference? It is not that I feel sorry for men. I do not mind if they have lost out. It is rather that it will be of no benefit to us women in the long run if we continue to do the wrong thing. We must push men out in other areas – in professional and public life. In those areas I am in favour of any ruse, even deception. Every inch of ground gained there is a victory, and in that field we will always be competing to push men out (there is always room for them in the home by the stove). But in sexuality? If feminism is really the legitimate revival of female egocentricity, then should it not be the sort of egocentricity which can be accepted as the centre of certain male desires and which should even reach out for male potentiality as if for a tribute which it is owed? Renunciation after all was the name of the game for women in the bourgeois world – then why must feminism renounce even more by scorning the only gift which the male sex is prepared to offer to the female sex of its own free will?

But one thing at a time.

I have admitted that the women's movement was right in calling a halt. After this, women could have developed various new ideas. The idea of a kind of female sexuality where men played no part, or at most a very marginal part, was only one of many possible alternatives.

For many people, it would have been more promising to have a try at *equality* in sexual relations. That would have required us to remove the imbalances caused by male domination, instead of doubling them by an equally one-sided female subversion. Using a rather worn-out but still dignified terminology: such an approach would have led to a conception of sexuality as being a 'union of male-female activity and passivity'. It would have avoided isolating the sexes from one another and it would have gone on to relativize the peculiarities of each sex which have been *fixed* ('fate' in the Freudian sense). Such an approach would have thrown a critical light on the practical reality which had come down to us, showing it to be one-sided, reductive, impoverished and cowardly, but not identifying it with 'male sexuality' (whose shortcomings had to be counterbalanced by constructing a better 'feminine' sexuality).

I maintain that sexuality was 'originally' arranged in accordance with the needs of both sexes and that it only satisfies the needs of one sex if it also satisfies the needs of the other. If that is correct, there can be no such thing as gender-specific sexuality. If *both* sexes are represented in this realm of pleasure and pain which we call sexuality, with all their demands and rights and all that they are willing and able to do, then one sex cannot be deprived without the other suffering a loss. It would then be impossible to cheat women out of their pleasure without also stealing something from men, just as it would not be admissible to reserve fulfilment for men only or for women only. Either both sexes would have to stride through this realm or neither would, at least as far as its full dimensions are concerned. Pleasure would be indivisible.

If feminist criticism had gone in this direction, it would have given men an idea of *how much* they are missing if they degrade sex to a relationship of domination, denying women the right to express their desires and press for fulfilment. Because if my assumption is correct, the fulfilment of female desire would enrich men in turn.

So what are these female desires? The 'blueprint' excludes the possibility of men fulfilling women's desires, at least men as they were until very recently. The blueprint demands female lovers or changed male lovers. It seems to me legitimate to demand that men must change if they want to come into the reckoning as lovers once more. But what direction should this change take?

The 'blueprint' remains vague on this point. On the one hand, it demands more empathy from men. On the other hand, it does not consider them capable of giving this. Basically, the feminist idea of 'female sexuality' remains hostile to men: it is intended to make it clear to them that things cannot continue as they are, yet at the same time it does not specify which (new) direction should be taken.

A need for vengeance and an understandable hatred for male arrogance may have been responsible for the tone of this blueprint. It has had the desired effect – many men feel in some way 'insecure' now. Of course, it is fun to see these self-important beings at a loss, but in the long run this fun is no substitute for a skilful lover. So let us try to suggest the direction in which men could/should change – we will then get back indirectly to women's desires.

In sexuality, it is my thesis that the sexes are in a relationship of *reciprocal interdependence*. A relationship of reciprocal interdependence cannot at the same time be a relationship of domination – unless it is in the sense that the sexes take it in turns to dominate one another or that both are dominated by sexuality. It is well known that the patriarchy managed to distort the relationship and to turn it into one of domination. It did not restrain the male craving for dominance even where this became *damaging* to the patriarchy itself or to the male sex as a whole. There was a double price to pay for dominating women in sexuality. We know the price women had to pay: they had to sacrifice their desire, their activity and part of their pleasure. And what about men? The price they had to pay is clear from the list of sacrifices made by women. By seldom being desired, too seldom propositioned, and seldom provoking or witnessing female lust, the price they had to pay was that their narcissism, and their ability to be passive wasted away, as did their sexual pride as far as this is nourished by providing pleasure. These costs were also borne by women (for what use is a lover who cannot give himself completely to a woman; whose own arousal is not dependent on him producing desire and giving pleasure, etc.), as generally in sexuality every deficit on one side returns as a loss for the other. Since these costs are borne by women too, it seems to me that it is advisable for men to change, to become more narcissistic, prouder and more passive (not in the sense of indifference, but by allowing things to be done to them sensually).

If we may reconstruct women's desires from these notions of

change, then we can say that women (as autonomous lovers aware of their desires and capabilities) want to feel their desire, or 'wait for it' and then be able to *show* it (the connection between having and showing desire is such that a desire which cannot be expressed does not develop and hence does not exist at all). They want to be able to be active, i.e. not only reacting but also provoking reactions; they want to have their pleasure. This point is admittedly rather sensitive. Because it is difficult to determine which agents take female pleasure from its inception to full expression, the feminist blueprint of a female sexuality with laws of its own has a high standing. If I succeed in clarifying this point to some extent, I will have proved my thesis that 'sexuality is a realm for both sexes or for neither', that 'pleasure is indivisible'. It will then be clear that so-called female sexuality is a mirage. I'll see what I can do.

The central issue of the 'blueprint' in the early seventies was the *relativization of the penis*. It was said that the penis was secondary or even unsuited for the job of satisfying women. Since then the penis has competed with female or male tongues, fingers or dildoes as equally valid tools of love. It has forfeited its dominant role for female pleasure, if I interpret things correctly, in the programmes of the various avant-gardes which express an opinion on this subject (the women's movement, lesbians, gays, the alternative movement and other subcultures). As far as sexual practices in the narrower sense are concerned, it may well be that other variants beyond penetration have become more widespread.[1] So much the better – a desire to experiment leads to development and refinement in sex too. But if we now want to consider sexuality as it is considered in the feminist blueprint as a field of human behaviour and expression with its social norms, symbolic ways of communicating and mental dynamics (and not merely techniques in the narrower sense) then we must emphasize other things.

I wrote the above to prevent a misunderstanding: in my opinion there can never be a great enough variety of practices and alternative forms of sexuality. It is these practices above all which contribute to the development of a 'sexual culture'. Putting them into practice requires manipulating the parameters of pleasure – a *conditio sine qua non* for a process of 'cultivation'. Nevertheless variety and refinement do not negate the existence of an organizational centre, a main focus or a basic pattern – on the contrary, they presuppose such a centre (by continually referring to it as they vary, alter, shift or defamiliarize in some other way). The focus which female desire seeks is, I maintain, the penis. It has the decisive lead in the 'competition' to satisfy women's instincts. It was not because of this organ that women had (and have) such great difficulties in finding pleasure in heterosexual coitus, nor was it because of the existence or dominance of a clitoris allegedly out of reach of the penis.

It was and is because of the patriarchal asymmetry which has distorted sexuality and has made it practically impossible for either sex to give *while* also taking and to see the other sex as a polar contrast in the sense of a complement, continually defining, relativizing and challenging it. When a friend asked me recently what women needed to be satisfied I answered 'the penis'.[2] I was immediately accused of 'phallocentricity' (by a man!). I replied that I could not help it because it is sexuality which is phallocentric. And of course it is only half phallocentric: it is just as much 'vaginocentric'. I really should not have to emphasize this point because, after all, the one sexual organ is nothing without the other. The one *makes* the other. The phallus only becomes what it is when it sees, expects or imagines the vagina – or an equivalent: the hollow of the hand, the mouth or the hollow of the knee for that matter. It is only itself as long as it is enclosed by the vagina (or an equivalent). In this sense, you can say that the phallus is the product of the vagina, that the vagina produces it, that the vagina creates it. The vagina for its part is the product of the phallus, it is only itself when seeing, expecting or imagining the phallus – or an equivalent, be it a finger, a tongue or a dildo. The phallus creates it by causing it to open; and it only remains itself, broadening and sucking, as long as the phallus (or an equivalent) is in front of it or in it.

That sounds very simple, but it is only simple as long as the people involved consciously assume that the sexes and their organs rank as equal and affirm this equal ranking with their sexual practices. It is well known that no such assumption is made. The male sex overestimates what it has and what it can give, and underestimates what it does not have (i.e. what the female sex has).

The female sex overvalues that which it does not have – and has now, in its rebellion as a women's movement, overreacted and declared what it had rated too highly to be totally irrelevant, at the same time undervaluing what women have. The way out of this problematic situation is, I think, *not* to shift the asymmetry in favour of the female side (wrong moves ruin the whole game in the long run), but to restore the symmetry, i.e. equality.

I hope this will be understood. Symmetry implies that each sex is proud of its particular attributes which the other sex perceives and desires as being something it lacks. In that way it is able to see the other's attributes as equal to its own. Yet symmetry also implies that each sex is *not just* tied to its own particular attributes in a restrictive way, but that each sex has potential attributes of the other sex within it, a kind of '*shadow sex*'.

This prerequisite for an exchange of roles in sexuality makes the boundaries between the sexes *fluid*: and only by being fluid can they be *fixed* once more. Only if the male part begins to realize that the female part is a possibility that it too can adopt (and even actually imitate) will it be able to perceive and play out a clearly distinguished (and therefore reduced) male role. Only if the female sexual role has the male sexual role in its blood will it feel and enjoy its femininity as one pole and as a restricted (in the sense of concentrated) experience. Men who are considered to be well versed in the art of love always have their 'feminine sides'. In most cases, they know something about passivity, i.e. they are able to appreciate and enjoy female aggression and to 'receive' pleasure. Any man who has not felt the pleasures of surrender will never really achieve very much in the practical *ars amandi*. The reverse is true for women.

We could also put it as follows: the very 'male' men and the very 'female' women (in the sexual sense), lovers who are imaginative and open to new experiences, are in most cases somehow *bisexual*. This homoeroticism may be, and usually is, directed towards the self only, a kind of narcissistic pleasure in the arousal which one's own body is able to provoke. (This kind of narcissism has traditionally been fostered to excess in women while it is often non-existent in men. By the same token, women have not in most cases developed a readiness to take in the attractions of the other sex with all their senses, while men's willingness to do this is blown up beyond any limits of decency. These are the consequences of male domination.)

Let us look at another example of this quite particular symmetry where the two sides complement one another but can also replace one another. During the sex act itself, if successful, it is no longer possible for the aroused senses to tell which body is which, where the phallus begins and the vagina ends. This blurring of the boundaries then again provides the basis upon which we can *identify decisively* with our own sex in *those* moments of coitus where such identification is required: at the beginning and the end. Or, to look at it another way, by radically feminizing the woman and masculinizing the man, it is then possible at certain crucial points in the sex act to enter the sphere of fluid boundaries or even of an exchange, feminizing the man and masculinizing the woman. The scheme is simple, but in practice it is difficult to achieve. In all cases it is the restrictiveness of roles which interferes.

Even early on, the women's movement was to some extent aware of a need to develop the (opposite) 'shadow sex' within itself and consistently insisted on the clitoris being the female sexual centre. The existence of a mysterious erogenous zone with no biological function is a good indication of the 'double-sidedness' of each individual sex. But instead of bringing in the clitoris as proof of the irrelevance of 'penetration', women (or women *and* men) ought to have looked for a male equivalent of the clitoris, a kind of male vagina which may not exist in anatomical terms but which nevertheless plays a significant part in the physiology of orgasm. I am convinced that there is such a thing – even if it is only a mental representation. But no one has dared approach this taboo, the taboo of feminizing men, which is one of the oldest pillars of the patriarchy. So what would be the result of feminizing men? Not the softy – the softy was a result of the old Freudian question 'What does woman want?' and he confined himself to caressing alone to be on the safe side. No, feminizing men in the sense of activating the 'shadow sex' would mean making men learn *passivity*, the ability to *receive* pleasure (instead of always only getting it). If men succeeded in learning this, masculinity would acquire more distinct contours at the same time (because sexual self-awareness depends on activating the 'shadow sex'). The ability to receive pleasure would seem to be the latent other side of the manifest male aggression in sex. Incidentally, the more refined *hommes à femmes* know this and cultivate its more delicate appeal.

I suspect that it was male aggression which neither feminists nor open-minded men were able to cope with. Men had discredited themselves too far by violating and battering women for their aggression to be accepted, where it might have some 'point', by injured women and 'insecure' men. Yet aggression is an indispensable part of sexual pleasure. For both sexes. On this point, sexuality offers an opportunity to sublimate aggression: under the law of sexuality, a 'useful' kind of aggression is possible. There aggression serves directly the cause of peace (of satisfaction). Yet it is possibly difficult to handle aggression 'in the right way'. It is also difficult to talk about it without becoming indignant or remaining clinically neutral. Would it not be a slight on all raped and mistreated women to stimulate male sexual aggression in word and deed?

First of all, the brutality of a rapist (or even of a wife-batterer) should not be seen as *sexual* activity. Men insist on this interpretation in order to salve their consciences, they know very well that their motives have nothing to do with sexual love. Thus criticizing the breakdown of sexual mores brought about by men, rebelling against misery in the bedroom, as justified as this may be, is no use if it is based on unrealistic assumptions. It is unrealistic to postulate a fluid feminine sexuality which was intended, on the basis of certain untruths, to transform the erotic ritual with its threatening temptation for both sexes to transcend boundaries, into boundless harmony. Pleasure cannot be had so easily: 'peace' (satisfaction) involves a risk, requires a kind of 'militancy'. Instead of wanting to eliminate aggression as being a male evil, the women's movement and the inheritors of the sexual revolution ought instead to have looked for new norms and modes of expression which would have allowed women to express their own sexual aggression.

Aggression in sex is not a male monopoly. There are enough myths or mythical images which point to a collective consciousness of female sexual aggression, ranging from the Amazons to the *vagina dentata*. It was probably only modern bourgeois society with its

tendency to domesticate women which first castrated the female sex
so completely and which first implanted a model of docile female
sexuality with so much success that we ourselves have since come
to believe in it. The male 'shadow sex' within us permits us to use
direct aggression, just as our manifest femininity has contributed
its own pulling and engulfing force. The tendency of both men and
women to identify aggression with the male sex organ alone,[1] the
primitive overrating of this organ in general, demonstrates to
me that the sexual consciousness prevailing in our culture is at an
infantile level. Should the penis *alone* be the incarnation of sex just
because it is easier to get hold of and to see? Little children let their
imagination be guided by what is clear to see: for them bigger
equals better. Only gradually do they learn to think in terms of
relations and correlations and to take account of what is not
immediately visible when forming their judgements and intentions.
How long will it be before we as sexual beings grow up?

 Female aggression cannot be fully formed as an active sexual
element, as a nuance in eroticism, until men have begun to learn to
be passive. That is clear. The interdependence forced upon the
sexes by sexuality imposes certain limitations on the good will
which each sex can show in an effort to change its behaviour. The
retreat of women to their own kind – in every other field an
important prerequisite for the revival of female egocentricity – was
of rather limited benefit in sexuality. Talking about it together may
have done women some good, but what then? Women discovered
the clitoris, but this discovery did not change them psychologically.
They could have utilized the discovery to try out (hetero-)sexual
aggressivity. Instead they were only concerned with looking after
this organ and incorporating it into the same old female passivity
(which of course has its own beauty, but which alone, without an
active and aggressive counterpoint, is virtually running idle). The
clitoral orgasm is the product of stimulation carried out with the
utmost delicacy. The man (if he was given a part to play at all),
ashamed of his aggressiveness, learnt this art, and the result was
the softy. I have nothing against men (and women) who know the
finer points; but in sexuality, so to speak, the dialectic never ends. I
have the suspicion that only those who also do the rougher things
are really able to do the finer ones.

'Female sexuality' in the feminist Utopia, the great flood of pleasure, etc., was a one-sided radicalization of the female role and of female physiology, an idling narcissism which did not get us very far, a phantom. All disavowed aggression was heaped onto men, and men were then excluded unless they were prepared to learn how to be gentle (a lesson which might have done them good, by the way). Women's existence suddenly took on boundless dimensions, a depth beyond consciousness and they thought they were independent from men. But what is a sea without ships?[3] Granted, men's piracy had gone too far, precluding any thought of an agreed settlement. But what about female instinct? After all, it really does exist. If women do not stop invalidating its object, they will damage that instinct instead of developing it. Women do not have to regard the caricature men have made out of their own sexual role as the limit of the female instinct's potential.

The subcultural atmosphere in which a discussion like this flourishes (and to which we owe a lot) is not favourable to a programme or an alternative plan such as mine. Out of the criticism of the meritocracy and out of the Utopias of the alternative movement, there has developed a kind of pacifist lethargy which scarcely realizes any longer that even peace can be irreconcilable and which, for its wholesome enjoyment, wants a kind of defused sexuality which can be practiced casually on the side. It is common knowledge that the price of this idyll is a permanent quasi-therapeutic grumbling by people to one another and the dulling of all passions. In opposition to that, there is the dream of spontaneity and directness, but again people are not prepared to pay anything to realize it and so it remains a dream. Yet this dream is powerful enough to pass a verdict on the calculated and refined aspects of sexual relations which may still be justified, and would in fact be part of a sexual culture.

But apart from the subculture – even the wider current trends do not augur well for a beneficial revolution in relations between the sexes. Women are hurt too deeply, and men as a sex have weighed themselves down with too much objective guilt for there soon to be a 'militant peace' between the sexes. It is possibly unavoidable that the two sexes will prolong even further the rest they are taking from one another until, if things go well, at some time one has faith in the covetous glance of the other. In this situation, the idea of a specifically female sexuality, of a female capacity to experience an endless chain of climaxes may be some consolation – but it is no substitute for that one climax which is enough in itself.

Notes

1   A word which has always annoyed me because it is unfortunate semantically it two respects. First it is not really appropriate since 'penetration' really means 'breaking through'. The penis breaks *in*, but not even the strongest one comes out again somewhere else (which would amount to 'breaking through'). Secondly, the fact that 'penetration', despite being inappropriate, enjoys such popularity as a word shows that feminists, no less than macho males, tend to ascribe a magic power to the male sex organ.

2   The idea that heterosexual genital patterns are 'basic' does not, I stress, imply that other pleasure-inducing techniques or homosexuality are in any way inferior. It is not intended to set up a hierarchy of pleasures or pleasure-giving organs. It merely fixes the centre from which the – then autonomous – variations originate. It is not more' than a statement about a general structure (i.e. one governing all possible variants), and which does not apply in individual cases.

3   At the same time, it is clear from the start that a ship is nothing at all without an ocean . . .

Index